Taxation of Income from Domestic and Cross-border Collective Investment

Andreas Oestreicher • Markus Hammer
Editors

Taxation of Income from Domestic and Cross-border Collective Investment

A Qualitative and Quantitative Comparison

Prepared by
Andreas Oestreicher and Sebastian Bause

With support contributed by
Anne Höfner, Timm Klare, Reinald Koch,
Jens Prassel, Florian Schmiedl, and Dirk Stiefel

Editors
Andreas Oestreicher
Faculty of Economic Sciences, Business Administration, Tax Division
University of Göttingen
Göttingen
Germany

Markus Hammer
Wirtschaftsprüfungsgesellschaft, Financial Services Tax
PricewaterhouseCoopers AG
Frankfurt am Main
Germany

ISBN 978-3-319-00448-8   ISBN 978-3-319-00449-5 (eBook)
DOI 10.1007/978-3-319-00449-5
Springer Cham Heidelberg New York Dordrecht London

Library of Congress Control Number: 2013943917

© Springer International Publishing Switzerland 2014
This work is subject to copyright. All rights are reserved by the Publisher, whether the whole or part of the material is concerned, specifically the rights of translation, reprinting, reuse of illustrations, recitation, broadcasting, reproduction on microfilms or in any other physical way, and transmission or information storage and retrieval, electronic adaptation, computer software, or by similar or dissimilar methodology now known or hereafter developed. Exempted from this legal reservation are brief excerpts in connection with reviews or scholarly analysis or material supplied specifically for the purpose of being entered and executed on a computer system, for exclusive use by the purchaser of the work. Duplication of this publication or parts thereof is permitted only under the provisions of the Copyright Law of the Publisher's location, in its current version, and permission for use must always be obtained from Springer. Permissions for use may be obtained through RightsLink at the Copyright Clearance Center. Violations are liable to prosecution under the respective Copyright Law.
The use of general descriptive names, registered names, trademarks, service marks, etc. in this publication does not imply, even in the absence of a specific statement, that such names are exempt from the relevant protective laws and regulations and therefore free for general use.
While the advice and information in this book are believed to be true and accurate at the date of publication, neither the authors nor the editors nor the publisher can accept any legal responsibility for any errors or omissions that may be made. The publisher makes no warranty, express or implied, with respect to the material contained herein.

Printed on acid-free paper

Springer is part of Springer Science+Business Media (www.springer.com)

Preface

Collective investment is a form of joint participation in shared assets. Unlike a direct investment where securities or other assets are acquired directly by the investor, in this case the investor places the funds at the disposal of an investment company or a mutual fund via a collective investment. It is the task of the investment company to invest the liquid funds received from the investor in risk-diversifying manner, for example in stocks, bonds, or real estate, according to investment principles agreed upon in advance. The form of the collective investment from the civil law perspective determines the legal relationship between the investor and the investment company and, thus, also on whose account the funds are invested by the investment company.

It therefore follows that with respect to taxation, various different levels (assets, investment property, and investor) have to be considered in this context. Special domestic tax provisions are normally in place for investment property. In particular, the possibility exists that the collective investment is treated as a company and, hence, as a tax subject where certain conditions are fulfilled but is rendered tax-free (transparent).

The investor who, as a natural or legal person, is subject to income or corporate income tax must declare his or her income from the collective investment, under special provisions if applicable. Should the facts and circumstances of the case lead to the application of the transparency principle, the investor is treated in principle as though he or she had received the income directly and without interposition of the collective investment. Both distributed and retained earnings are deemed to be taxable income. When it comes to detail, the question is which investment strategies are concerned. Typically, the differentiation in this context is between stock funds (dividends and capital gains), bonds and money market funds (interest), real estate funds (rent or lease and capital gains), speculative transaction funds, and other funds (for which special domestic treatment applies, such as favorable treatments for pension funds, for example).

Although in principle the resulting tax consequences are clear, it emerges that numerous special circumstances, which furthermore differ significantly from country to country, are to be observed in individual cases. If one seeks to determine tax advantages or to check whether there is a need for tax reforms, one quickly comes to the conclusion that a comparison of alternative investments is no easy task. Against this background, the subject of this study (which has its origins in a corresponding request from the Ministry of Finance of Hessen) is to examine the tax treatment of investment income, including the legal framework conditions (requirements according to the legal form and regulatory provisions) in an international comparison. Here we distinguish between the tax consequences to be considered at the various taxation levels (assets, collective investment, and investor). Of particular interest is also the issue of whether collective investment vehicles as such are entitled to apply double taxation agreements in their own right or make use of corresponding double taxation agreements on behalf of their investors.

In locational terms, our comparison covers France, Germany, Italy, Ireland, Luxembourg, the Netherlands, Switzerland, the UK, one Asian country (Japan), one Scandinavian country (Denmark), and one Eastern European country (Poland). Our analysis of the relevant tax provisions, which is of primarily qualitative nature, is complemented by a quantitative comparison of the tax burden for a model investor investing assets nationally in the form of a collective investment.

If one limits one's attention to languages most widely used across Europe, it becomes clear that the information necessary in order to set up a comparison of this kind is not available in the literature in sufficient depth. In particular, such information does not exist in a uniform and comparable form for the group of countries under consideration. For this reason, we requested the international accounting firm PwC AG to support the project by providing the necessary data via its international network.

Among other things, this study is based on three degree theses (one Bachelor thesis, one Master thesis, and one diploma thesis) written by students in the tax division of the Faculty of Economic Sciences at the *University of Göttingen*. The Master thesis of *Anne Höfner* and the Bachelor thesis of *Timm Klare* deal with the differing national tax systems for taxation of income from collective investment in selected countries and give a qualitative international comparison. The thesis by *Anne Höfner* places a special focus on the cross-border context. In his Diploma thesis, *Florian Schmiedl* puts forward a quantitative comparison of the tax burden on income from investment property held domestically and across borders with respect to the selected group of countries.

In designing the concept of these theses and in their supervision, we were supported in highly constructive manner by Dr. *Reinald Koch*, who also made valuable contributions to the quantitative analysis. We are grateful to *Jens Prassel* for his work in consolidating the results and conducting parts of the analysis. He also drafted the presentations and analyses for the country chapter. In this work, he was supported by *Josip Oreskovic-Rips*, tax adviser with PwC AG. *Sebastian Bause* performed the task of processing this extremely complex and complicated material for purposes of the analysis, which is based on information from highly diverse cultures and legal systems. He also proposed a second draft and adjusted it to legal changes taking place in the meantime. *Sebastian Bause* was supported by *Dirk Stiefel* of PwC AG, who contributed a section on the "treaty entitlement" of funds. The idea behind our study was proposed by *Friedrich Brusch*, head of the tax department at the Ministry of Finance in Hessen. We are grateful to his members of staff *Matthias Schenk, Andreas Rolker, Fabian Röhrich*, and Dr. *Alexander Mann* for their constructive remarks and the discussion of this survey's design. The study could not have been accomplished without the input of PwC. In particular, we would like to thank Prof. Dr. *Dieter Endres* and Dr. *Hans-Ulrich Lauermann* for their invaluable support.

Göttingen, Germany　　　　　　　　　　　　　　　　　　　Andreas Oestreicher
Frankfurt am Main, Germany　　　　　　　　　　　　　　　　Markus Hammer
March 2013

List of Abbreviations

AFM	Autorité des marchés financiers (French financial supervisory authority), Autoriteit Financiële Markten (Dutch financial supervisory authority)
AIF	Authorized Investment Fund
AO	Abgabenordnung (General Tax Act)
Art.	Article
AUT	Authorized Unit Trust
BB	Betriebs-Berater (Journal)
B.V.	Besloten Vennootschap
Ch.	Chapter
CH	Confoederatio Helvetica (Switzerland)
CII	Capital Investment Institution
CIT	Corporate Income Tax
CNMV	Comision Nacional del Mercado de Valores (Spanish financial supervisory authority)
COLL	Collective Investment Schemes Sourcebook
CONSOB	Commissione Nazionale per le Società e la Borsa (Italian financial supervisory authority)
CSSF	Commission de Surveillance du Secteur Financier (French financial supervisory authority)
CV	Commanditaire vennootschap (Dutch legal form)
DB	Der Betrieb (Journal)
DBA	Doppelbesteuerungsabkommen (Double Tax Treaty)
DE	Deutschland (Germany)
DFSA	Danish Financial Supervisory Authority
DK	Dänemark (Denmark)
DKK	Dänische Krone (Danish Crown)
DStR	Deutsches Steuerrecht (Journal)
DTA	Double Tax Agreement
DTT	Double Tax Treaty (Doppelbesteuerungsabkommen)
e.g.	Exempli gratia (for example)
ed.	Editor

edn.	Edition
EFG	Entscheidungen der Finanzgerichte (Journal)
etc.	Et cetera
ES	Espagna (Spain)
EStG	Einkommensteuergesetz (Income Tax Act)
EU	European Union
FBI	Fiscale Beleggingsinstelling (Dutch fund type)
FCP	Fonds Commun de Placement (French fund type)
FGR	Fonds voor gemene rekening (Dutch fund type)
FI	Fondo de Inversión (Spanish fund type)
FINMA	Eidgenössische Finanzmarktaufsicht (Swiss financial supervisory authority)
FR	France
FSA	Financial Services Authority (UK financial supervisory authority)
GDP	Gross Domestic Product
GewStG	Gewerbesteuergesetz (Trade Tax Act)
HBR	Herbeleggingsreserve (reserve for re-investment according to Dutch tax law comprising of retained earnings at fund level)
ICG	Informal Consultative Group
IE	Ireland
IMF	International Monetary Fund
InvG	Investmentgesetz (Investment Act)
InvStG	Investmentsteuergesetz (German Investment Tax Act)
IRPEF	Imposta sul Reddito delle Persone Fisiche (Italian regional surcharge on the tax on income of natural persons)
IStR	Internationales Steuerrecht (Journal)
IT	Italy
JP	Japan
KStG	Körperschaftsteuergesetz (Corporation Tax Act)
LU	Luxembourg
MTC	Model Convention (with respect to taxes on income and on capital)
n/a	Not applicable, not available
NL	The Netherlands
no.	(Marginal) number
N.V.	Naamloze Vennootschap (Dutch legal form)
OECD	Organisation for Economic Co-Operation and Development
OEIC	Open-end(ed) Investment Company (UK fund type)
p.	Page
PIF	Professional Investor Fund (Irish fund type)
PL	Poland
PP	Private property
QIF	Qualifying Investor Fund (Irish fund type)
QIS	Qualified Investor Scheme (UK fund type)
REITS	Real Estate Investment Trusts
RIC	Regulated Investment Company (US fund type)

List of Abbreviations

S.A.	Société anonyme (French legal form)
S.A.R.L.	Société à responsabilité limitée (French legal form)
S.C.A.	Société en Commandite par Actions (French legal form)
SICAV	Société d'Investissement à Capital Variable (French fund type), Società di Investimento a Capitale Variabile (Italian fund type), Sociedad de Inversión de Capital Variable (Spanish fund type)
SIF	Specialised Investment Fund
SIT	Securities Investment Trust (Japanese fund type)
UCITS	Undertakings for Collective Investment in Transferable Securities
UK	United Kingdom (Great Britain and Northern Ireland)
USA	United States of America
UT	Unit Trust (Anglo-American fund type)
VBI	Vrijgestelde Beleggingsinstelling (Dutch fund type)
VCIC	Variable Capital Investment Company (UK fund type)
Wft	Wet op het financieel toezicht (Dutch Financial Supervision Act)
WHT	Withholding tax

Contents

1 Introduction 1
   1.1 Motivation 1
   1.2 Subject Matter of the Investigation and Definitions 3
   1.3 Approach 4
   Reference 5

2 Analysis 7
   2.1 Contextual Basis 7
      2.1.1 Overview of Relevant Structures in Investment Taxation ... 7
      2.1.2 Fund Types and Taxation 9
      2.1.3 Agreement Entitlement of Funds 11
   2.2 Taxation of Income from Investment Funds 19
      2.2.1 Overview 19
      2.2.2 Taxation Consequences at Asset Level 22
      2.2.3 Consequences of Taxation at the Fund Vehicle Level (Fund Level) 26
      2.2.4 Consequences of Taxation at Investor Level 41
      2.2.5 Concluding Remarks on Investment Taxation in the Domestic Case 52
      2.2.6 Taxation of Income from the Disposal of Fund Units ... 56
      2.2.7 Draft Reform Proposal for Public Fund Investment Taxation in Germany 58
   2.3 Quantitative Comparison of Tax Burdens 60
      2.3.1 Overview 60
      2.3.2 Research Methods 61
      2.3.3 Model Assumptions 61
      2.3.4 Discussion of Calculation Results 66
      2.3.5 Analysis of the Tax Effects Linked to the German Draft Reform Proposal 72
   2.4 Summary 77
   2.5 Annexes 78
   References 89

3	**Country Summaries**		91
	3.1	Sources of Information	91
	3.2	Tabular Representation	91
		3.2.1 Denmark	91
		3.2.2 Germany	96
		3.2.3 France	101
		3.2.4 Ireland	106
		3.2.5 Italy	110
		3.2.6 Japan	113
		3.2.7 Luxembourg	118
		3.2.8 Netherlands	123
		3.2.9 Poland	128
		3.2.10 Switzerland	131
		3.2.11 Spain	135
		3.2.12 USA	140
		3.2.13 United Kingdom	144
	References		149

List of Symbols

$C_{(F)WHT}$	Credit at fund or investor level of (foreign) withholding tax withheld at asset level
$C_{F(I)}$	Credit at investor level of withholding tax withheld at fund level
F	Separate taxation of returns at fund level
F(I)	Withholding tax on returns at fund level on the account of investor
I	Separate taxation of the investor
$T_{[country]}$	Tax rate applied by the country [country]
–	No tax consequences at the corresponding level
r_t	Profitability in year t
r	Pre-tax internal rate of return on investment in a fund
r_s	Net-of-tax internal rate of return on investment in a fund
s	Effective tax burden arising from investment in a fund

List of Figures

Fig. 2.1 Representation of investment structures examined in the "domestic case" (basic case) 20
Fig. 2.2 Representation of investment structures examined in "cross-border case 1" 21
Fig. 2.3 Representation of investment structures examined in "cross-border case 2" 21
Fig. 2.4 Representation of investment structures examined in the "three-country-case" 22

List of Tables

Table 2.1	Fund types investigated in the countries selected	10
Table 2.2	Withholding tax rates at asset level in the domestic case	23
Table 2.3	Withholding tax rates at asset level in international cases pursuant to unilateral regulations	25
Table 2.4	Tax liability and taxable entity status of funds in the field of income tax and other taxes in the domestic case	27
Table 2.5	Consideration at fund level of withholding taxes withheld at asset level in the domestic case (basic case and cross-border case 2)	30
Table 2.6	Consideration at domestic fund level of foreign withholding taxes withheld at asset level in the international case pursuant to unilateral regulations (cross-border case 1 and three-country case)	31
Table 2.7	Offsetting losses for tax purposes at fund level in the domestic case	33
Table 2.8	Obligation to distribute the income earned to the investors in the domestic case (basic case and cross-border case 1)	34
Table 2.9	Withholding tax deduction at fund level on behalf of the investor in the domestic case (basic case and cross-border case 1)	35
Table 2.10	Withholding tax deduction at fund level on behalf of the investor in the international case pursuant to unilateral regulations (cross-border case 2 and three-country case)	38
Table 2.11	Impact of profit appropriation policy at fund level on the tax liability of the investor (basic case and cross-border case 1)	42
Table 2.12	Determinants of income qualification at investor level	46
Table 2.13	Consideration at investor level of domestic withholding taxes withheld at asset level in the domestic case	48
Table 2.14	Consideration at investor level of domestic withholding taxes withheld at fund level in the domestic case (basic case and cross-border case 1)	49

Table 2.15	Consideration at investor level of foreign withholding taxes withheld at asset level in the international case pursuant to unilateral regulations (cross-border case 1 and three-country case)	50
Table 2.16	Consideration at investor level of foreign withholding taxes withheld at fund level in the international case pursuant to unilateral regulations (cross-border case 2 and three-country case)	51
Table 2.17	Characterisation of the investment tax systems examined	53
Table 2.18	Taxation of profits from the disposal of fund units in the domestic case	57
Table 2.19	Calculation of the pre-determined tax base	60
Table 2.20	Differentiation of situations in the course of quantitative analysis	62
Table 2.21	Overview of the parameters of the quantitative model	67
Table 2.22	Lowest and highest effective tax burden for fund units in personal assets	68
Table 2.23	Effective tax burden for fund units in business assets	70
Table 2.24	Overview of effective tax burdens	73
Table 2.25	Comparison of effective tax burdens of fund investment in Germany under current tax law and under the draft reform proposal	75

Introduction

1.1 Motivation

Existing forms of collective investment of capital address different groups of investors and in many cases are tailored to their specific needs. These fund structures are essentially characterized by two main features. Firstly, several different structures are possible in legal terms. These vary considerably from country to country. Secondly, fund structures often display a distinctly international orientation; in many cases funds address investors around the globe and invest the capital made available in international investment assets. As a rule, the investments are not limited to the country where the funds are based. From this it follows that the fund structures result in highly complex taxation issues, raising numerous problems in detail and matters of doubt. This holds especially with respect to cross-border taxation issues. Due to the vast number of fund vehicles operating in the various countries, it is scarcely possible for an investor to determine at a glance which investment is tax optimal from his or her particular perspective.

Against this background, in conducting this study we pursue two main goals. The first is to carry out a compact and systematic comparison of the most important income tax consequences of private investments in publicly available funds operating at important fund locations in Europe, America, and Asia (details concerning the subject matter are to be found in Sect. 1.2 below) and which are structured in accordance with the European UCITS directive or are comparable to it. This comparison allows us to determine the central common features or differences between the taxation concepts of the various countries (Chap. 2). To this end, summaries in table form and diagrams are designed to facilitate accessibility of the information. Our second goal is to supply information on the country-specific taxation concepts in a targeted and user-friendly way. A brief description of the national tax system applicable to funds is provided. Moreover, the chief tax consequences are set out using a uniform table format. A presentation of the country-specific taxation concepts is given country by country in a separate chapter (Chap. 3).

The present study, therefore, features the following three specific aspects. First, the comparative analysis in Chap. 2 allows us to observe what the 13 major tax regimes have in common and where they differ when it comes to taxation of funds. To the best of our knowledge, a comparative view covering such an extensive range of countries has not been carried out up to now. Second, the comparison of national tax burdens reveals valuable indications concerning the attractiveness of investment locations for natural persons subject to unlimited income tax liability[1] and enable initial conclusions to be drawn with respect to possible reforms in fund taxation. Third, the country-specific presentation in Chap. 3 provides an overview of investment income taxation at selected important fund locations. In this way, the reader can gain quick access to information regarding main features of fund taxation in the 13 countries under consideration in this study. Hence, this chapter serves as an introduction to fund taxation in these countries.

The structure of this study is as follows. Chapter 2 is devoted to the comparative analysis. In order to achieve enhanced comprehensibility uniform terminology is used as far as possible for all countries. A brief explanation of the most important terms is given in the following Sect. 1.2. The beginning of Chap. 2 is given over to a depiction of some main principles of fund taxation. Section 2.1 provides a brief overview of the relevant taxation levels which give rise to tax consequences, a discussion of the characteristic fund types is carried out, and the question of a treaty entitlement of the various fund types is addressed. Section 2.2 considers taxation of income from investment funds. In this context, the taxation on the asset level ("asset level"), the level of the collective investment ("fund level"), and at the level of the investor ("investor level") is considered separately, whereby a distinction is made in each case as to whether the investment is purely domestic or cross-border. Moreover, taxation of income from sale of fund units is discussed; here, too, the taxation of the purely domestic and cross-border situation is presented separately. In Sect. 2.3 the alternative and country-specific tax burdens are calculated and presented in comparative manner. This presentation of the methodological instruments applied in the study is followed by discussion of the model assumptions and calculation results. A brief summary of the most significant results of our research rounds off the analysis in Sect. 2.4. The presentation in Chap. 3 deals with fund taxation in the individual countries. A brief description is followed up by a tabular representation of current tax provisions at fund level, at investor level, and upon sale of the individual assets or fund units.

---

[1] For methodological reasons the groups of institutional investors and cross-border fund-structures of considerable significance in practice cannot be taken into account in the framework of the quantitative analysis.

1.2 Subject Matter of the Investigation and Definitions

The study deals with publicly traded funds meeting the requirements of the UCITS directive (for example in terms of the investment law in Denmark, France, Germany, Ireland, Italy, Luxembourg, the Netherlands, Poland, Spain, Switzerland, and the UK). In addition fund structures in Japan and the USA were given consideration, provided they are comparable with publicly traded funds corresponding to the UCITS directive.

Regarding the legal design of the collective investment, a fundamental distinction can be made between a "contract type" and a "company type". In the case of a contract type, in return for his input of capital the investor receives a unit certificate in the collective investment, whereby the collective investment remains separate from the corporate property of the investment company; in this alternative the legal relationship is consequently defined via the investor's contractual claims vis-à-vis the investment company. Contrastingly, in the case of a company type the investor obtains a direct share in the investment company itself. Furthermore, in this case there is no distinction between the corporate property of the investment company and the collective investment. For the safe-keeping of the assets in both cases, a depot bank independent of the investment company is generally utilized. This bank is also responsible for issue and repurchase of units/shares and exercises a control function but has no influence on the tax provisions to be applied. It can only carry out procedural functions within the taxation framework (for example, paying withholding tax to the tax authorities). These two basic forms of fund can vary in detail in their design from country to country. For example, investment funds situated in the non-mainland European countries and the Anglo-American countries are often designed using trust structures related to the "contract type".

Up to now, the "company type" has been employed to a clearly lesser extent than the "contract type" in Germany. According to statistics published by the BaFin ("Bundesanstalt für Finanzdienstleistungsaufsicht", German Financial Supervisory Authority) concerning admissible investment trust companies (contract type) and investment corporations with variable capital (company type), the company type makes up a proportion of only 23 % on November 15, 2011.[2] As far as taxation is concerned both types are treated identically in Germany. However, this is not the case in all countries investigated, nor is there always such a clear preference for one fund type as is the case in Germany. Consequently, both forms are observed in the countries concerned in the course of this study.

For purposes of our calculations at investor level only domestically resident natural persons subject to unlimited income tax liability ("retail investors") are considered. The latter can hold their fund units/fund shares in private assets or in business assets, in as far as this distinction is relevant. Investments made by corporations are excluded from this study. The same applies for institutional

---

[2] Cf. German Financial Supervisory Authority (2012).

investors, such as insurance companies. The investigated case group is further limited by the fund's investment portfolio. We look at investments in bonds (for example fixed interest securities) and shares (for example shares in stock corporations or listed companies), so from the tax perspective the study is focused on interest, dividends, and capital gains. Therefore, in the framework of the qualitative analysis we scrutinize domestic and cross-border income taxation both at fund level and investor level and any withholding taxation, including its treatment at either fund or investor level. Non-income-dependent taxes and taxation of fund management are excluded from consideration. Our quantitative analyses are limited to the purely domestic case, the identifying feature of which is that the investment is made in a fund located in the investor's country of residence. Cross-border investment structures, however, cannot be modelled in general due to the fact that the tax consequences depend to a large extent on the individual case. The dependence prevents us from being able to achieve any reliable determination of cross-border tax burdens.

For the sake of simplification and in the interests of a comparative review, the following terms are defined and employed in the further course of this report. In the framework of our study "fund", "investment fund" and "fund vehicle" are employed as generic terms for all forms of collective capital investment that fulfill the requirements of the UCITS directive or—in the case of Japan and the USA—are comparable with these. The question of their regulatory and company law basis and the precise legal form of the vehicles or issuing companies both have no bearing on this labeling. As a consequence, both the vehicles set up as a company (company type) and those based on contract (contract type) or those in the form of a trust (trust type) are termed "funds". In line with this definition, "fund shares" or "fund units" refer to the respective shares or units in the corresponding capital investment vehicle.

"Domestic investors" are natural persons who are resident or are deemed resident in the country in whose jurisdiction the fund concerned was set up. "Foreign investors" are natural persons who are resident or deemed resident in a country other than the country in which the fund concerned was set up.

"Assets" is the term given to the investment objects in which the fund invests. We consider investments in shares and obligations, the returns on which basically give rise to income from interest, dividends and capital gains upon sale of these assets.

1.3 Approach

Our point of departure is the distinction between the purely domestic case on the one hand and the cross-border case on the other. The pure domestic case is characterized by the fact that domestic investors invest in domestic assets via domestic funds, i.e., investors, funds, and assets are subject to the same tax jurisdiction. In the cross-border set-up, the investor's country of residence is a country other than the country in which the fund is based. In this cross-border set-up we distinguish between cross-border case 1, cross-border case 2, and the "three-country-case". In cross-border case 1 the assets are subject to a different tax jurisdiction to that of both the fund and the investor. Cross-border case 2, however, refers to situations in which assets and fund have a common tax jurisdiction, whereas the investor is resident in another country. In the "three-country case", assets, investment fund, and investors all fall under different tax jurisdictions.

In order to demonstrate and assess the various set-ups, it is necessary to know the tax regulations of the investment countries concerned. It was not possible in the context of this investigation to acquire the necessary information using primary source and secondary literature only. In the interests of compiling a reliable, complete and comparative data basis, we therefore found it necessary to gather information directly. This survey is based on a standardized questionnaire and was carried out with the support of the international PricewaterhouseCoopers network of tax accounting and auditing firms. Unless otherwise indicated the data presented here applies as of December 2010.[3]

The relevant regulations differ very considerably from country to country and cannot be presented in detail in this report. Nevertheless, we considered it necessary to provide a brief description of the taxation systems, the legal bases, and taxation at fund and investor level. This information is given in table form, ordered country by country, and can be found in Chap. 3 of this report. In addition to presenting the regulations pertaining to the purely domestic case, we also look at the special features that are significant for the cross-border case (at fund level under the heading "specific characteristics of foreign assets/investors" and at investor level "special characteristics of the foreign fund"). If several fund types are to be distinguished in any particular country we refer to them individually.

Reference

German Financial Supervisory Authority (2012) List of admissible investment trust companies and investment corporations with variable capital. http://www.bafin.de/SharedDocs/Downloads/DE/Liste/Unternehmensdatenbank/dl_li_kag_invag_zugel.xls?__blob=publicationFile&v=1. Accessed December 15, 2012

---

[3] In principle, in the majority of countries observed no significant changes in investment taxation law relevant to the present study have since taken place. Exceptions apply in the case of Italy and the UK which is why the legal status of July 2012 is referred to here. Moreover, as far as Germany is concerned, the legal status as of March 2013 is applied due to recent changes in the taxation of dividend income accrued to publicly traded investment funds.

Analysis 2

2.1 Contextual Basis

2.1.1 Overview of Relevant Structures in Investment Taxation

2.1.1.1 Approaches to Taxing Income from Collective Investment

In principle, tax consequences can arise at three taxation levels, that of the investor, the investment fund, and the assets. How investment taxation is applied in the individual case depends first and foremost on the means employed by the tax legislator to achieve the intended taxation outcome.

In this context taking an economic perspective the question arises as to the number of levels the tax legislator identifies as separate tax payer with the ability to pay tax on income received. Potential candidates are the investor him/herself and the fund. In practice three situations are conceivable. In the first, individual ability to pay is only attested to the investor while the fund itself is not regarded as being taxable. The second option is that only the fund but not the investor is assigned its own tax subjectivity. And finally, the tax legislator can also take the view that both the investor and the fund are separately liable to taxation.

From a legal perspective the tax legislator has various instruments at its disposal to achieve the intended taxation outcome. In order for the tax legislator to subject the tax payer to liability according to the latter's ability to pay, the tax payer is typically made liable to income tax on his or her entire worldwide income. Besides this tax assessment procedure, taxation of an investor's earnings from capital is frequently taxed at source (withholding tax). In this situation, the payer of return on capital is obliged to withhold tax on the account of the recipient for remittance to the tax authorities of the source state; hence only the net returns on capital pass to the recipient. In the cross-border context, this upfront taxation serves to secure the tax payer's limited tax liability in the source state. In the domestic context, however, the withholding of tax merely constitutes a particular form of collecting income tax which is actually only due in the course of tax assessment.[1]

In order to avoid taxing the same income twice over at the level of the tax payer, it is usual to apply methods to avoid double taxation according to which the tax withheld in advance is either credited against the tax due as assessed or deducted as income-related expense. Alternatively, the income already taxed at source is excluded from income tax assessment.

All the countries included in this study are united in seeing the investor's separate ability to pay as given. They consequently subject the return on capital to tax also on the part of the investor. On the other hand, tax treatment of funds varies considerably among the countries examined. We can distinguish between the three systems outlined in the following.

2.1.1.2 No Separate Ability to Pay on the Part of the Fund
Transparency Approach and Pass-through Taxation of the Investor
Where the fund is seen as not having a separate ability to pay, one possibility is to attribute the investment income earned at asset level directly to the fund investor for tax purposes. Accordingly, for tax assessment of the income, the fund level then becomes irrelevant. All transactions that were actually carried out at fund level are, for tax purposes, to be deemed as not to have taken place or are to be accounted for in such a way as to eliminate accrual of income at fund level.

"Interimistic" Taxation at Fund Level
From the administrative point of view, any consistent implementation of pass-through taxation is a highly challenging business. A more practical approach to taxing the fund in a transparent manner is to apply an "interimistic" taxation. This involves not "looking through" the fund to the investor as is the case in transparent taxation, but, as a first step, taxing the fund itself. If it is ensured by way of suitable measures that the additional tax burden arising at the level of the fund from such separate fund taxation is fully neutralized at the investor's level, from the economic perspective this brings about the identical result as would be achieved via transparent taxation.

2.1.1.3 Separate Ability to Pay on the Part of the Fund
Where the fund is deemed to be an economic subject to which a separate ability to pay is to be attributed, in addition to the investor also the fund is liable to separate income tax. Should there be no procedure according to which this taxation is

---

[1] In order to apply a uniform terminology, the term "withholding tax" is understood in its tax systematic context and, thus, will not only be used in the cross-border situation but applies also to the purely domestic situation. On this note the German "*Kapitalertragsteuer*" is referred to more generally as (domestic) withholding tax on capital, for example.

neutralized (for example, by way of imputation) a classic case of "economic double taxation" arises, since the investment income accrued from the investment objects is subject to a twice-over income tax burden.

2.1.2 Fund Types and Taxation

2.1.2.1 Contract Type
In the case of a contract type the invested capital is pooled as separate property, the ownership of which lies either with the investment company in its fiduciary capacity or with the investors in the form of co-ownership. The consequence is that the separate property does not possess its own legal personality. In the interest of protecting the investor, the separate property is held in a custodial account separately from the property of the investment company at an independent depot bank which is also responsible for the issuing and buying back of fund units, and which assumes a control function. The investors conclude a contract for service with the investment company which administers the separate property and makes investment decisions.

2.1.2.2 Trust
The trust is an Anglo-American legal form with a structure comparable to that of a German "Stiftung" (foundation). In a "fiduciary form" it closely resembles the contract type. When compared to the latter, however, a crucial difference lies in the fact that the invested capital and the resulting income are in the ownership of the trustee. The latter is entrusted with administering the capital and the income in accordance with the rules set out in the "Stiftungsurkunde" (foundation certificate) for the benefit of the investor.

2.1.2.3 Company Type
In the case of the "company type" investment capital is not separated from the corporate property of the investment company. The initiators of the fund participate in the variable corporate equity and the business property of the investment company limited as so-called "voting shareholders", just as the investors do as so-called "non-voting shareholders", whereby the latter forego their participation and voting rights. Hence, the invested capital is property of the investment company limited and is administered by this company in its own name and on its own account. Investment administration can be carried out by an external contracting party. As with the contract type, an independent depot bank assumes custodial and control functions and manages the issuing and buying back of fund units.

2.1.2.4 Realization of the Varying Fund Types
The fund types outlined above are in use to a varying extent in the countries considered here. Table 2.1 shows to which basic type the investment funds,

Table 2.1 Fund types investigated in the countries selected

Country	Legal designation of the investment fund[a]			Legal design
Denmark	Investeringsforening			Company type
Germany	Sondervermögen			Contract type
	Investmentaktiengesellschaft (InvAG)			Company type
France	Fonds Commun de Placement (FCP)			Contract type
	Société d'Investissement à Capital Variable (SICAV)			Company type
Ireland	Unit Trust (UT)			Trust type
	Variable Capital Investment Company (VCIC)			Company type
Italy	Fondo Comune di Investimento (FCI)			Contract type
	Società di Investimento a Capitale Variabile (SICAV)			Company type
Japan	Shōken tōshi shintaku			Contract type
				Company type
Luxembourg	Fonds Commun de Placement (FCP)			Contract type
	Société d'Investissement à Capital Variable (SICAV)			Company type
Netherlands	Fonds voor gemene rekening (FGR)/Commanditaire vennootschap (CV)			Contract type
	Fiscale beleggingsinstelling (FBI)	Besloten vennootschap (BV)		Company type
		Fonds voor gemene rekening (FGR)		Contract type
		Naamloze vennootschap (NV)		Company type
	Vrijgestelde beleggingsinstelling (VBI)	Fonds voor gemene rekening (FGR)		Contract type
		Naamloze vennootschap (NV)		Company type
Poland	Open-ended Investment Fund			Company type
Switzerland	Fonds Commun de Placement (FCP)			Contract type
	Société d'Investissement à Capital Variable (SICAV)			Company type
Spain	Fondo de inversión (FI)			Contract type
	Sociedad de Inversión de Capital Variable (SICAV)			Company type
USA	Open-end Management Company			Trust type
				Company type
United Kingdom	Authorized Unit Trust (AUT)			Trust type
	Open-ended Investment Company (OEIC)			Company type

[a]The fund types listed here are those selected to quantitative analysis

which are regulated differently from country to country, are to be allocated. In countries where use of different fund types is possible, distinctions between fund types are referred to in the following only insofar as they are relevant for taxation purposes.

2.1.3 Agreement Entitlement of Funds

2.1.3.1 Issue
Agreement entitlement of funds has always been considered controversial. The issue comes up regularly as to whether a fund that invests in assets to which a different tax jurisdiction applies than to the fund itself can claim the benefits of the double taxation agreement (DTA) between the country in which the fund is located and the source country. So it must be determined whether a fund itself is protected by the agreement. If this is the case, the fund can apply for a refund of the withholding tax retained beyond the agreed withholding tax rate in the source country. In addition, certain source countries offer funds covered by the DTA the opportunity to apply in advance for reduced withholdings. If the reduced withholding tax rates pursuant to the DTA are applied, the net asset value (NAV) of the fund increases and thus the value of the shares outstanding held by the investors.

If the fund itself does not qualify to be covered by the DTA, the extent to which the DTA considers investors to be the beneficial recipients of the fund profits should be examined. Then a "transparency principle" would apply. However, with retail funds, a refund claim at investor level is eliminated for purely practical reasons in the sense of the UCITS directive; the shares are often held by thousands of investors and the funds invest in many different countries. So a potential refund at investor level will not be examined here.

2.1.3.2 Agreement Entitlement in General
Overview
The OECD model tax convention (OECD MTC) specifies that a fund can only reap the benefits of a DTA between the country where the fund is located and the source country in its own right when the fund qualifies in the contracting state as a "resident" and as the "beneficial owner" of the income.[2]

In the following section the agreement requirements are each briefly explained and, on this basis, the extent to which these requirements apply to the three types of funds to be examined (company type, contract type, trust type).

The Term "Person"
Article 3, par. 1(a) of the OECD MTC defines "person" to mean individuals, companies and any other bodies of persons. Since the qualification of being a natural person does not apply, it should be determined whether the fund qualifies as a "company" or a "body of persons".

One difficulty is that each of the countries considered has its own legal forms for setting up a fund. So in the process of determining whether a fund is a person in the

---

[2] OECD is the abbreviation for the Organization for Economic Co-operation and Development. In order to support its member countries with the wording of double taxation conventions, OECD experts are engaged in developing model tax conventions.

sense of the OECD MTC definition, the legal types should always be compared first.³ However, the very different composition of these entities in the various jurisdictions often makes comparison difficult.⁴

Company
Article 3 par. 1(b) of the OECD MTC defines "company" as juridical persons or legal entities treated as juridical persons for tax purposes (so-called quasi-judicial persons).

The term juridical person should essentially have the same meaning in the domestic tax law of the parties to the agreement (country in which the fund is located and source country). "Juridical persons are social entities to whom the legal system grants legal capacity to the same extent as to natural persons," meaning they are recognized as independent legal bodies. Tax law ties into this legal capacity.⁵

The term quasi-judicial persons covers e.g. non-incorporated firms or trusts that have independent tax liability or can opt to be taxed according to corporation tax law. It also includes German *Sondervermögen* that are considered by fiction of law for tax purposes to be an independent entity subject to corporation tax.⁶

For the purpose of the DTA, it is decisive that the juridical person or the quasi-judicial person either benefits from actual taxable entity status or could benefit from potential taxable entity status. On the other hand, personal or factual tax exemption in one of the contracting countries is irrelevant.⁷

Company type funds should always qualify as juridical persons and thus have taxable entity status. This is why these funds should generally qualify as a company in the sense of the OECD MTC.⁸

Contract type funds are not juridical persons in the sense of the definition.⁹ But if they are taxed as such (quasi-juridical person), they are essentially to be considered to be a company as defined by the OECD MTC. However, there can be conflicts in qualification if the fund is taxed as a juridical person in the one contracting country, but is considered a transparent entity for tax purposes in the other country. In this case the other country will not recognize the fund as a quasi-juridical person in the sense of the DTA because of the lack of taxable entity status. If such conflicts in qualification occur, Article 3 par. 2 of the OECD MTC states that the legal personality should be interpreted pursuant to the domestic law of the state applying

---

³ Cf. Haase (2009), p. 631.

⁴ Cf. Zinkeisen (2007), p. 584, refer also to Table 2.1 herein, which attributes the fund types used in the countries observed to the three basic fund types identified.

⁵ Cf. Vogel and Lehner (2008), Art. 3 no. 13.

⁶ Cf. Vogel and Lehner (2008), Art. 3 no. 15; Berger et al. (2010), Sect.11 InvStG no. 3.

⁷ Cf. Debatin and Wassermeyer (2012), Art. 3 DTC no. 18; Sorgenfrei (1994), p. 472; Zinkeisen (2007), p. 583 et seq.; Aigner (2001), p. 102.

⁸ Cf. Vogel and Lehner (2008), Art. 3 no. 13; Schmidt (2002), p. 649; Geurts and Jacob (2007), p. 737 et seq.

⁹ Cf. Debatin and Wassermeyer (2012), Art. 3 DTC no. 19.

the DTA (applying state). So the fund must be able to have taxable entity status from the point of view of the applying state. It must be hypothetically envisaged how the respective legal form in the source country would be taxed if that form were to earn taxable income.[10] German *Sondervermögen*, which do not have their own legal personality but are taxed as juridical persons in Germany, are sometimes denied DTA access, the reasoning being that the applying state does not consider them to have taxable entity status, because they deem them to be a transparent entity for tax purposes.[11]

Funds set up as trusts are generally considered by Anglo-American law to have a legal personality and, under certain conditions, are treated as juridical persons for taxation purposes. Consequently they can definitely qualify as a company in the eyes of the country of domicile.[12] However, conflicts in qualification can still occur. The legal form of a trust is not common outside of the Anglo-American judicial area, and non-Anglo-American countries could deem the trust to be transparent for tax purposes when the legal forms are compared. But a vehicle considered by the country of jurisdiction to be transparent for tax purposes can never qualify as a company as defined by the OECD MTC.[13]

Other Body of Persons
The OECD MTC does not provide a definition for an "other body of persons". But since all juridical persons fall under the definition of a company, the argument can be reversed to state that only entities can be considered that on the one hand fulfil the requirements to be seen as persons in the sense of the treaty and on the other hand have neither legal personality nor have independent tax liability, meaning they are not taxable entities according to the law of the applying state. Some agreements exclude bodies of persons from the term "person".[14] Then an investment fund must qualify as a company to represent a person in the sense of the treaty.[15] If, on the other hand, the applicable agreement includes bodies of persons in the definition person, a contract type fund or a trust fund—to the extent that these two types of funds do not already qualify as companies based on existing taxable entity status in the applying state (see footnote 15)—should always be subsumed under the term body of persons and be classified as a person in the sense of the agreement.[16]

---

[10] Cf. Debatin and Wassermeyer (2012), Art. 3 DTC no. 19.

[11] Cf. Vogel and Lehner (2008), Art.1 no. 72.

[12] Cf. Vogel and Lehner (2008), Art. 3 no. 15; Kronat (2002), p. 124 et seq., p. 142 et seq.

[13] Cf. Kronat (2002), p. 128 et seqq.; Debatin and Wassermeyer (2012), Art. 3 DTC no. 19; OECD (2009), p. 10.

[14] Cf. Vogel and Lehner (2008), Art. 3 no. 17, 25; Debatin and Wassermeyer (2012), Art. 3 DTC no. 20; Kronat (2002), p. 103.

[15] Refer to section "Company".

[16] Cf. Kronat (2002), p. 129.

The Term "Residency"
In Article 4 par. 1 of the OECD MTC, a resident is defined as a person residing in a contracting country who, according to the law of the country, is liable to tax therein by reason of his/her domicile, residence, place of management or any other criterion of a similar nature.

A person is a resident of a contracting country when he/she is subject to unlimited tax liability in that country and thus qualifies as an independent taxable entity. Article 4 par. 1 refers to domestic law of the country of residency. The person must be able to prove the location-related properties that justify resident taxation in accordance with the domestic law of the country.[17] Potential tax exemption of the fund should not have any effect on its taxable entity status.[18] It depends on the existence of an abstract personal tax liability. This is the result of the interpretation of the regulation from the context, particularly from its function as one of the requirements for application of the allocation norms of the agreement. Allocation of taxation between the contracting countries ties into the person's residency. There need only be a relationship or personal relation to the country of residency that *can* lead to unlimited tax liability.[19]

However, conflicts in qualification may arise as well, if the contracting countries evaluate a person's personal tax liability differently.[20] Some countries disallow the taxable entity status of a fund in the country of residency if the fund is personally tax-exempt there.[21] This more literal interpretation of Article 4 par. 1 OECD MTC and specifically the term "liable to tax" contradicts the previously mentioned general understanding of residency according to *Wassermeyer*.[22] Furthermore, the tax exemption at fund level should be viewed in light of the elimination of double taxation at investor level (comparable to the regulations for taxation of publicly held stock corporations and their stockholders). The credit method or partial income

---

[17] Cf. Vogel and Lehner (2008), Art. 4 no. 76 et seqq.; Debatin and Wassermeyer (2012), Art. 4 DTC no. 29.

[18] Cf. Debatin and Wassermeyer (2012), Art. 4 MTC no. 25; Lang (2000), p. 527, 530.

[19] Cf. Vogel and Lehner (2008), Art. 4 no. 82 et seq.; Debatin and Wassermeyer (2012), Art. 4 DTC no. 1 et seq.; Aigner (2001), p. 52.

[20] Cf. Debatin and Wassermeyer (2012), Art. 4 DTC no. 1.

[21] Also refer to Finanzgericht Niedersachsen of March 29, 2007 6 K 514/03, p. 737 with regard to DTT Germany-France; for a critical assessment refer to Geurts and Jacob (2007), p. 737.

[22] Cf. Debatin and Wassermeyer (2012), Art. 4 DTC no. 25; Zinkeisen (2007), p. 584; Schmidt (2002), p. 649; Geurts (2011), p. 573; Lang (2000), pp. 527, 530; for a concurring view please also refer to Finanzgericht Rheinland-Pfalz of June 15, 2011 1 K 2422/08 concerning DTT Germany-France and Bundesfinanzhof of June 6, 2012 I R 52/11 concerning DTT Germany-France. The BFH, however, raises the question to what extent from a German perspective for French tax purposes a French SICAV is to be seen at least partially as tax transparent and insofar tax residency is to be denied on the grounds of lacking subjectivity to tax. The Court has passed the case back to the Rheinland-Pfalz tax court in order to clarify this issue. For a critical assessment affirming tax residency see Staiger and Köth (2012), p. 2915 et seq.

procedure at investor level often applies here, because—unlike with most funds—actual taxation occurs at the publicly held company level itself.[23]

Company type funds as juridical persons should always qualify as taxable entities in the country of residency.[24]

Contract type funds taxed as juridical persons in the country in which they are located[25] should be considered to be "resident" in the sense of the OECD MTC. On the other hand, contract type funds that can be considered completely transparent for tax purposes are generally not taxable entities. They may be considered to have a legal personality as specified by the DTA[26] but still not be covered by the agreement for reasons of residency, which always requires legal personality or taxable entity status.[27]

When a trust has been created in an Anglo-American country, it must be examined whether the trust is treated as an independent taxable entity or if, for tax purposes, the unit holders of the trust are directly affected. In general, a trust should qualify as a taxable entity according to Anglo-American law and therefore be considered to be "resident" in the sense of the OECD MTC.[28]

However, as explained above, when the term "liable to tax" is interpreted literally by the applying state, residency can be refused to all three types of funds due to personal tax exemption at fund level.[29]

The Term "Beneficial Owner of Yields"

According to Article 10 (Dividends) and Article 11 (Interest) of the OECD MTC, the privileges that the DTA offers should be granted only when the person invoking the benefits is the beneficial owner of the dividends and interest. In the prevailing opinion of relevant literature, the foundation for the term *beneficial owner* is independence of the status as formal property holder (*substance over form*). Only the person/entity with unlimited access to the object and its products can be the beneficial owner.[30] Transferring this concept to a retail fund means that the fund's management must have the freedom to decide whether assets are to be disposed of and in which way the realised liquidity is to be re-invested in other assets.[31] It is crucial that the "person" does not simply act as a conduit for third parties actually

---

[23] Cf. Zinkeisen (2007), p. 585; Sorgenfrei (1994), p. 465 et seqq.

[24] Cf. Wassermeyer (2001), p. 201.

[25] See section "Company".

[26] See section "Other Body of Persons".

[27] Cf. Kronat (2002), p. 146; Vogel and Lehner (2008), Art. 4 no. 73; Schmidt (2002), p. 648 et seqq.; Wassermeyer (2001), p. 200.

[28] Cf. Debatin and Wassermeyer (2012), Art. 3 DTC no. 19; OECD (2009), p. 10 et seqq.

[29] Cf. Debatin and Wassermeyer (2012), Art. 4 DTC no. 1 et seqq.

[30] Cf. Vogel and Lehner (2008), Vor Art. 10–12 no. 11 et seqq.; Debatin and Wassermeyer (2012), Art. 10 DTC no. 69.

[31] Cf. Vogel and Lehner (2008), Vor Art. 10–12 no. 11 et seqq.; Debatin and Wassermeyer (2012), Art. 10 DTC no. 68; Meinhardt (2003), p. 1783; Zinkeisen (2007), p. 584.

receiving the income, such as is e.g. the case with intermediate representatives, other agents or brokerage firms. When dividends are paid out, this means specifically that the fund has membership rights to the distributing company when a resolution on the profit utilization (distribution or rentention) is passed or—in the case of interest—that the fund can decide on the provision of capital, the use of the profits or both. This should generally be the case with the UCITS funds to be examined here.[32] This should not be affected by certain limitations of the freedom of decision due to specific investment requirements, mandatory distributions, etc. dictated in the fund's prospectus.[33]

Even if the criterion of beneficial ownership in regard to funds is sometimes still discussed controversially,[34] a retail fund as recipient of the income should always be a beneficial owner in the sense of the OECD MTC if he is taxed as the recipient in his country of residency. Apart from that, this is a prerequisite for residency in the sense of the OECD MTC.[35] Consequently, the types of funds examined here should always qualify as beneficial owners of the interest and dividend income when they are "residents" as defined by the OECD MTC.

2.1.3.3 Current Developments

Due to the conflicts in qualification and lack of clarity described in Sect. 2.1.3.2, there still exists a high degree of uncertainty in regard to the agreement entitlement of a fund. Tax-related uncertainties are always problematic for investment decisions. In regard to investments in fund units, this applies particularly in light of the fact that the retail funds examined here generally have to be appraised daily to determine the value of their units outstanding. Anticipated claims for withholding tax refunds are theoretically to be factored into determination of the NAV as an increase in value as early as at the time that entitlement is established, namely on the day that the withholding tax is withheld. The daily NAV forms the basis for determination of the issue and redemption prices. So if a claim to a withholding tax refund as a result of the DTA is entered in financial reporting and then in the following period is not actually refunded due to the described uncertainties, the determined amounts of the issue and redemption prices were incorrect in the meantime because they were inflated. This means that investors who redeemed or purchased units during this time received or paid too high a price. The opposite effect occurs when claims for refunds are not entered in financial reporting when the entitlement occurs due to the described uncertainties but are entered later, when actual payment is received.[36]

---

[32] Cf. Zinkeisen (2007), p. 584 with reference to Debatin and Wassermeyer (2012), Art. 10 DTC no. 62; Vogel and Lehner (2008), Vor Art. 10–12 no. 18.

[33] Cf. Vogel and Lehner (2008), Vor Art. 10–12 no. 11 et seqq.

[34] For an overview of the differing positions see OECD (2009), Annex 1.

[35] Cf. Vogel and Lehner (2008), Vor Art. 10–12 no. 15a et seqq.; Kronat (2002), p. 182 et seqq.

[36] Cf. OECD (2010), no. 6.15.

Uniform Interpretation of the General Agreement Requirements for Funds by the OECD

It was precisely for these reasons that the OECD Committee on Fiscal Affairs (CFA) started a task force in 2006, the Informal Consulting Group (ICG), comprised of representatives from the financial industry and from the fiscal administrations of various OECD member countries. During the following period the ICG drafted suggestions for uniform interpretation of when a fund meets the agreement requirements described in Sect. 2.1.3.2 according to the OECD MTC.[37] After the interested public was asked to offer their views on the topic, the revised OECD MTC commentary was published on July 22, 2010. The commentary now includes, in a separate section, the agreement requirements for funds.

In regard to the legal personality of a fund, tax treatment of the fund shall now be indicative according to domestic law of the *country in which the fund is located*—and not, as thus far has been the case, particularly with conflicts in qualification, according to the law of the applying state. However, to facilitate explicit clarification, this shall be included in the respective DTA.[38]

In regard to the residency criterion, it is always the case that funds treated as completely transparent for tax purposes in the country in which they are located do not qualify as residents in the sense of the OECD MTC. Funds considered intransparent for tax purposes in the country in which they are located—meaning they are classified as taxable entities—shall in contrast also qualify as residents if they are tax-exempt or are granted tax benefits. In this context, the revised MTC commentary also points out the difficulty mentioned above in section 'The Term "Residency"': several OECD member countries are of the opinion that tax-exempt funds cannot be considered to be liable to tax as defined by article 4 OECD MTC and thus cannot per se be resident. In such cases the only option is to find an approach through bilateral negotiations.[39]

According to the concept of the OECD, the beneficiary ownership criterion should now always be met when a fund qualifies as a "resident" in the sense of the OECD MTC, assuming the managers of the fund can make investment decisions in the name of the investors with no restrictions whatsoever. According to their concept, an essential aspect here is that the activities of the fund and its managers are generally vastly different from those of a representative, other agents or a trustee.[40]

Agreement Entitlement at Fund Level in the Case of Specific DTA Regulations

The explanations presented in section "Uniform Interpretation of the General Agreement Requirements for Funds by the OECD" regarding funds, which were included in the OECD MTC commentary, are viewed as positive in the sense of a

---

[37] For a more detailed discussion, please see also the report by ICG (2009).
[38] Cf. OECD (2010), no. 6.10.
[39] Cf. ibid., no. 6.10–6.13.
[40] Cf. ibid., no. 6.14.

more uniform interpretation of the general agreement criteria in its applicability to funds, but there still remain uncertainties having to do with specific cases. This is why, in addition to the mentioned explanations regarding general application conditions, the ICG has put together concrete formulation suggestions for DTA regulations specific to funds in the OECD MTC commentary. The suggestions can be added to existing DTAs and included from the start in future DTAs. These special regulations are intended to clarify that a fund that domiciles in the one contracting country and receives income from the other contracting country always qualifies as a "resident" and as the "beneficiary owner" of the income in the sense of the agreement. The special types of funds of the two contracting countries covered by this preferential regulation should be named specifically to completely eliminate any ambiguity. In the same way, types of funds not granted protection by the agreement can be explicitly excluded from the application.[41]

All of the types of funds not named in these special regulations should continue to be governed by the general application regulations, described in detail in Sect. 2.1.3.2 above, and substantiated by the ICG in the revised OECD MTC commentary.[42]

As a possible measure to prevent abuse, the ICG believes that the respective contracting countries could agree that funds benefiting from protection by the agreement due to such specific regulations could claim the agreement privileges only proportionately, namely only to the extent that the investors behind the fund qualify as so-called "equal beneficiaries" (so-called "limitation-on-benefit" regulation). Then as soon as the share of the equal beneficiaries exceeds a certain percentage (limit), a refund for the whole amount could be granted. The respective contracting countries have to agree on who exactly is to be seen as an equal beneficiary. In the view of the ICG, one possibility would be to subsume under this term only such persons residing in the contracting country in which the investment fund is located.[43] This approach of proportionate refund as a factor of the portion of investors residing in the country in which the fund is located is not new to administrative practice (DTA Germany—France, DTA Germany—Switzerland, DTA Germany—USA).[44] As an alternative, the circle of beneficiaries could be widened to include persons residing in a third country with which the source country has a DTA that provides an effective and comprehensive exchange of information. Furthermore, the preferential tax rate of this DTA (DTA third country—source country) has to be at least as low as the rate that the fund can claim pursuant to the DTA country of location—source country.[45] The administrative hurdles that arise for retail funds when the attempt is made to check the agreement entitlement for each individual investor will not be dealt with in detail here.[46] The OECD is aware of this

---

[41] Cf. ibid., no. 6.21 et seqq.
[42] Cf. ibid., no. 6.16 et seqq.
[43] Cf. ibid., no. 6.26.
[44] For a detailed review, see Zinkeisen (2007), p. 583 et seqq.
[45] Cf. OECD (2010), no. 6.21.
[46] See ibid, no. 6.29 et seq.

issue and has in a separate OECD report compiled potential solutions as to how such a verification could take place with estimations applying statistical methods.[47] The OECD also suggests that funds traded publicly on the market should always be able to take advantage of the agreement benefits to the maximum amount, the reasoning being that risk of abuse by such funds can considered to be minimal.

With these pre-formulated fund-specific DTA regulations, a basic shift can be detected away from purely transparent treatment of funds for purposes related to the agreement and towards fundamental agreement entitlement of funds.[48] However, the ICG believes that the transparency principle could still be applied if the investors behind a fund were to be entitled to an even greater reduction in the withholding tax rate for direct investments, e.g. in the case of pension funds as investors.[49]

Since publication of the OECD report in 2009 and the subsequent revision of the OECD MTC commentary, many OECD member countries have already added fund-specific agreement regulations of the type described above to their DTAs. It is to be expected that in the future additional countries will follow these examples to eliminate the uncertainties related to the agreement entitlement of funds.

2.2 Taxation of Income from Investment Funds

2.2.1 Overview

In order to be able to carry out in a practical manner a tax-systematic investigation of the investment tax systems of the countries included—despite the complexity of investment taxation as already mentioned—this study is structured in the following according to locational aspects and taxation levels. Subsequently the results of the investigation which were obtained successively in this way are combined and assessed as a whole.

From a locational perspective, the analysis distinguishes between purely domestic and cross-border investment activities. Limiting this study to purely domestic investment activities would not take sufficient account of the incentives for investing internationally which are fuelled by the existing tax differentials in the international arena and today's high capital mobility. Accordingly, when considering the asset, fund, and investor level, in addition to presenting the tax consequences in purely domestic investment activities, we also look at the tax consequences that arise if (at least) one of these three relevant taxation levels is subject to a different tax jurisdiction.

---

[47] See OECD (2009).
[48] Cf. Geurts (2011), p. 574.
[49] Cf. OECD (2010), no. 6.28.

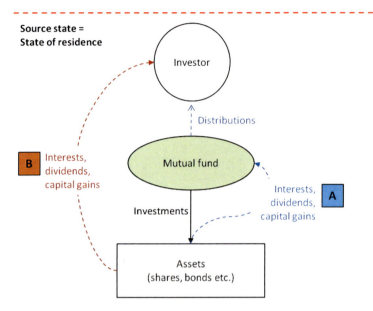

Fig. 2.1 Representation of investment structures examined in the "domestic case" (basic case)

Figure 2.1 provides a diagrammatic representation of the domestic case (basic case).

Here, as also in the cross-border situation, a fundamental distinction has to be made between the cases A and B. Case A refers to the situation in which funds are taxed according to the separate entity principle with the consequence that in principle two tax subjects exist in the person of the fund and in the person of the investor participating in the fund. In case B, in contrast, fund taxation is carried out according to the transparency principle. Here, fund taxation is ignored for tax purposes; instead income is attributed directly to the investor's income accrued from the investment assets.

Whenever presentation of the tax consequences calls for differentiation of cases A and B, we proceed in this way.

The cross-border situation also included in this analysis is illustrated in diagrammatic form below (Fig. 2.2). In the first cross-border case constellation, the source state, i.e., the state in which the investment income originates (state in which investment object is located) is not the state in which the fund and the investors participating in the fund are resident. This first variation on the basic case is termed "cross-border case 1" in the following.

Alternatively, the fund's state of residence and the state of location of the investment objects are identical, i.e., the fund is also resident in the source state, when the investors are resident in one other state which is not the source state. This variation on the basic case is termed "cross-border case 2" (Fig. 2.3).

In the final constellation, it is assumed that both in terms of receiving income, i.e., in relation to its investment objects, and in terms of distributing income, i.e., in relation

2.2 Taxation of Income from Investment Funds

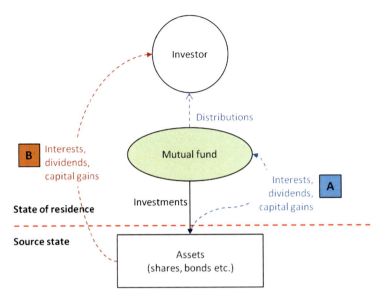

Fig. 2.2 Representation of investment structures examined in "cross-border case 1"

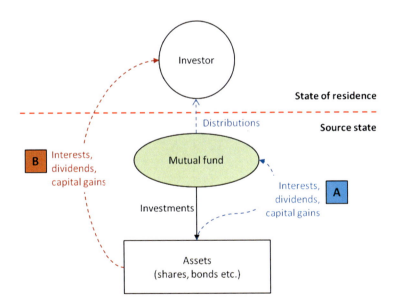

Fig. 2.3 Representation of investment structures examined in "cross-border case 2"

to its investors, the fund is a foreign entity (Fig. 2.4). Such a three-country-case may be seen as a variation on the basic case which does not need further elaboration here, since for discussion of its tax consequences reference can be made to cross-border cases 1 and 2.

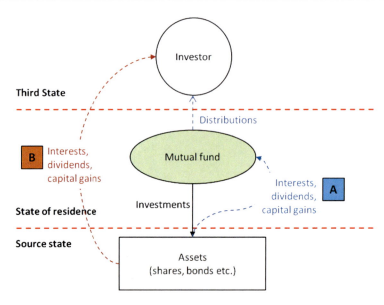

Fig. 2.4 Representation of investment structures examined in the "three-country case"

2.2.2 Taxation Consequences at Asset Level

2.2.2.1 Recipient of Investment Income Governed by Same Tax Jurisdiction ("Domestic Case")

If at asset level issuers of equity securities and bonds generate distributable investment income, a withholding tax liability may arise for the creditor of the investment income already at this level, where income from the assets flow into the fund. The motivation behind taxation in the form of withholding tax depends on whether it is a domestic or cross-border case.

In the case of purely domestic investments, the withholding tax is not an independent tax: withholding taxation is a specific form of income tax levied on the creditor involving taxation of gross investment income. When the fund is treated as intransparent (case A), this procedure serves as early application of corporation tax at the source of the investment income on behalf of the fund, which is regarded as the creditor of the investment income for tax purposes. If on the other hand funds are taxed according to the transparency principle (case B), the investor is charged income tax on the investment income that can be attributed to him for tax purposes in advance at the source of the income. The obligation to withhold tax on behalf of the creditor is borne in both cases by the party responsible for payment of the capital income.

If the assets are governed by a different tax jurisdiction than the creditor of the capital income earned from these assets (whether the fund or the investor), the country where the assets are located (source country) ensures with the withholding tax at asset level that the creditor fulfils his obligation to pay tax within his limited

2.2 Taxation of Income from Investment Funds

Table 2.2 Withholding tax rates at asset level in the domestic case[a]

Country where assets are located	Equity securities		Bonds		No withholding tax
	Current income	Capital gains	Current income	Capital gains	
Denmark	15 %/0 %	–	–	–	
Germany					X
France					X
Ireland					X
Italy	–	–	0 %/20 %/12.5 %	–	
Japan					X
Luxembourg					X
Netherlands	15 %/0 %	–	–	–	
Poland					X
Switzerland	35 %	–	35 %	–	
Spain	19 %	1 %	19 %/0 %	1 %	
USA					X
United Kingdom					X

[a]To the extent that amounts of holding are relevant for withholding taxation of capital gains, it is assumed that the "substantial participation threshold" is not reached

tax liability in the source country. Analogue to the domestic case, the domestic payer of the capital income is obligated to withhold tax on behalf of the foreign creditor.

Table 2.2 shows which countries charge withholding tax at asset level in domestic cases and how high the tax is. The table differentiates between income from equity securities and bonds, whereby there is more detailed differentiation for the two types of assets between current (ordinary) income in the sense of regular, recurring payments from holding the assets, and (extraordinary) profits from the disposal of these assets.

Equity securities Of the 13 countries examined, nine (Germany[50], France, Ireland, Italy[51], Japan, Luxembourg, Poland, USA, United Kingdom) refrain from charging withholding tax on income from equity securities. The range of tax rates charged in the other four countries is 0–35 %. In *Denmark* the rate depends on the type of entitled fund, whereby the regular domestic rate is 15 %. If however the income is attributed to a fund that opted for taxation under the special distributing

---

[50] When the fund submits a non-assessment certificate.

[51] Since January 1, 2012, Italian tax law has been applying a uniform withholding tax rate of 20 % to all income and capital gains from financial instruments. However, income earned by domestic funds from investments in domestic enterprises are exempt from the withholding tax.

fund regime[52], no withholding tax is charged at asset level. The generally applicable tax rate of 15 % in the *Netherlands* is reduced to 0 % when the equity securities are held by qualified, tax-exempt funds. *Switzerland* applies a tax rate of 35 % to current dividend payments (so-called *Verrechnungssteuer*, withholding tax); none of the other countries examined charge such a high tax at the source of such investment income. In *Spain* 19 % withholding tax is retained on all current dividend income. In addition, withholding tax at a rate of 1 % is charged on the profits gained by the fund from disposal of its equity securities.

Bonds When it comes to investment income gained from bonds, ten of the countries examined (Denmark, Germany, France, Ireland, Japan, Luxembourg, Netherlands, Poland, USA, United Kingdom) refrain from domestic taxation at the source. The frontrunner amongst the remaining three countries is once again *Switzerland*, with a 35 % withholding tax. The withholding tax of 19 % applied in *Spain* to current income from equity securities generally also applies to current income from bonds; in the case of government bonds, there is no withholding tax at all. Profits gained from the disposal of bonds are taxed at a rate of 1 %. Tax law in *Italy* generally provides extensive tax exemption on income earned by domestic funds; however, special provisions governing exceptional cases may explicitly dictate a withholding tax at the regular rate of 20 % at asset level or—with investments in government bonds—at the reduced rate of 12.5 %.

2.2.2.2 Recipient of Investment Income Governed by Other Tax Jurisdiction ("International Case")

When a cross-border case is examined in which the source country (the country in which the assets are located) is not the country of residency of the creditor of the capital income, it can generally be stated that the tax law of any country examined provides withholding tax rates independent from the country in which the creditor resides. Table 2.3 shows the type and scope of cross-border withholding taxation at asset level. It becomes apparent that, in an international case, taxation is noticeably more generalized and more comprehensive than in the domestic case. Specifically, the actual legal form of the fund located in the other country is usually not significant for withholding taxation, neither on the merits nor in terms of amount.

Equity securities Amongst the countries included in the study who basically apply a withholding tax to current income earned on equity securities, there is—as with the domestic case—a range of tax rates between 0 % and 35 %, whereby *Switzerland* is once again the forerunner. The *USA* deduct a tax of 30 % from the yields, while the rate of 28 % in *Denmark* is slightly less. In *Germany* and *France* 25 % is always withheld; however, in Germany a *solidarity surcharge*, an additional tax of 5.5 % of the actual withholding tax must also be paid, resulting in a

---

[52] Refer to the remarks on Denmark in country Chap. 3 for an overview of the requirements under which an investment fund can claim this special tax regime.

Table 2.3 Withholding tax rates at asset level in international cases pursuant to unilateral regulations[a,b]

Country where assets are located	Equity securities		Bonds		No with-holding tax
	Current income	Capital gains	Current income	Capital gains	
Denmark	28 %	–	–	–	
Germany	26.375 %	–	–	–	
France	25 %	–	–	–	
Ireland	20 %/0 %	20 %/0 %	20 %/0 %	20 %/0 %	
Italy	20 %	–	20 %/12.5 %	–	
Japan	20 %/7 %	–	15 %	–	
Luxembourg					X
Netherlands	15 %	–	–	–	
Poland	19 %	–	20 %	–	
Switzerland	35 %	–	35 %	–	
Spain	19 %	30 %/0 %	–	30 %/0 %	
USA	30 %	–	30 %/0 %	–	
United Kingdom	–	–	20 %/0 %	–	

[a]To the extent that amounts of holding are relevant for withholding taxation of capital gains, it is assumed that the "substantial participation threshold" is not reached
[b]In some cases double taxation agreements may prescribe lower tax rates

composite rate of 26.375 %. *Italy*, *Ireland* and *Japan* apply a regular rate of 20 %. Ireland waives the tax when the receiving fund resides in the EU, while Japan reduces the amount to 7 % when the income stems from publicly traded equity securities. There is no differentiation in the tax deduction at asset level in *Poland* (19 %), *Spain* (19 %) and the *Netherlands* (15 %).

In *Ireland* (20 %) and *Spain* (30 %) a limited tax liability is in principle also given for profit from the disposal of equity securities. However, there is no tax when a fund residing in the EU acts as a creditor.

Luxembourg and the *United Kingdom* do not apply withholding tax to current income generated from equity securities or to profits gained from the disposal thereof.

Bonds Seven of the examined countries basically apply a withholding tax on current income from bonds in the cross-border case. Switzerland applies a withholding tax of 35 % to such income, too. If the payer resides in the *USA*, he must always withheld a 30 % withholding tax, unless the interest flowing into the foreign fund stems from investments in US American banks or insurance companies, from bonds with an issue discount and a term of no longer than 183 days, from tax-exempt government-issued securities, or from portfolio bonds; no withholding tax is charged on such income. A rate of 20 % is fundamentally applied in *Ireland*, *Italy*, *Poland* and the *United Kingdom*. As with equity securities,

Ireland does not charge withholding tax on bonds when the fund resides in the EU. Italy applies a reduced rate of 12.5 % to income from Italian government bonds, while the United Kingdom grants a withholding tax exemption when proof is provided that the investors behind the fund are non-residents. Finally, in *Japan* a 15 % withholding tax is charged.

If the bonds are located in *Denmark, Germany, France, Luxembourg*, the *Netherlands* or *Spain*, the investing foreign fund is not subject to withholding tax.

In the international case, capital gains related to bonds can basically be subject to withholding tax in two countries. *Spain* withholds 30 % when the disposing fund does not reside in an EU country; in contrast, the fund is exempt from the tax when it is a resident of the EU. And *Ireland* applies the same principle to determine whether tax of 20 % is withheld.

2.2.2.3 Provisional Results

It is apparent that the withholding tax deduction at asset level is heterogeneous between as well as within the countries examined and that it depends on a few exceptions. The result of the different approaches in regard to tax transparency of investment funds is particularly a lack of uniformity on the issue of whether withholding taxes should be applied to the fund or to the investors behind the fund.

It is also striking that, in Denmark and the Netherlands, the withholding tax rate in the domestic case is a factor of which type of fund the creditor of income is. "Distributing funds" in Denmark as well as Dutch funds of the VBI type are tax-exempt entities (refer to Sect. 2.2.3) that cannot deduct withholding taxes at asset level or credit the taxes against their own tax debt. In this respect, it seems generally necessary that there is differentiation in the withholding tax rates and, in special cases, their reduction to 0 %. This means that investment income is taxed in Denmark and the Netherlands as if the intermediary funds did not exist.

2.2.3 Consequences of Taxation at the Fund Vehicle Level (Fund Level)

2.2.3.1 Independent Tax Liability of Fund

Taxation at the investment fund level will now be analysed. The countries in which funds are subject to independent income tax liability[53] must first be determined. In this context, the tax laws of the countries are examined to determine whether they allow tax losses to be offset at fund level. Then the issue will be examined as to whether the withholding taxes at asset level discussed in the previous section can be credited already at fund level and if so, how. And finally, it is of interest to discover

---

[53] In this context, the term "income tax" means an independent personal income tax that explicitly charges the investment funds according to their personal performance. It should specifically not be considered to be identical to income taxation of natural persons.

2.2 Taxation of Income from Investment Funds

Table 2.4 Tax liability and taxable entity status of funds in the field of income tax and other taxes in the domestic case

Country in which the fund is located		No independent tax liability		Independent tax liability	
		Not a taxable entity	Taxable entity	Income tax	Other tax
Denmark			X		
Germany	Dividends			15.825 %	
	Interest, capital gains		X		
France	FCP	X			
	SICAV		X		
Ireland			X		
Italy			X		
Japan	Contract type	X			
	Company type			42 %	
Luxembourg	FCP				0.05 %
	SICAV				0.05 %
Netherlands	FGR/CV	X			
	FBI			0 %	
	VBI		X		
Poland			X		
Switzerland		X			
Spain				1 %	
USA (RIC)				35 %	4 %
United Kingdom	Dividends		X		
	Interest			20 %	
	Capital gains		X		

the countries in which withholding taxes are charged on behalf of the investors at fund level, meaning when the income is distributed to the investors.

As Table 2.4 shows, independent income taxation at fund level occurs in only few cases. For income tax purposes, funds are prevailingly considered personal or factual tax-exempt entities.

Personal tax exemption is granted when the fund is not considered a taxable entity according to the country's regulations. This is often the consequence of a lack of independent civil legal personality and applies mostly to funds designed as civil contracts. This study indicates personal income tax exemption in France and Switzerland for funds with the legal forms SICAV and FCP, in Japan in the case of funds of the contract type, in Luxembourg with FCP and in the Netherlands with investment funds created as FGR and CV. In addition, funds can be exempted from income taxation even if they are considered to be taxable entities; in such cases the investment funds are granted factual tax exemption. Factual tax exemptions for funds exist in Denmark, Germany, France (SICAV), Ireland, Italy, Luxembourg (SICAV), the Netherlands (VBI) and Poland.

Germany applies a 15.825 % combined tax rate (corporate income tax and solidarity surcharge thereon) on dividend income derived by publicly traded investment funds. Interest and capital gains from the disposal of assets, however, are exempt from taxation at fund level.

Luxembourg does not tax income at fund level, but the net assets of the fund are subject to an annual 0.05 % subscription tax.

Amongst the countries that stipulate independent income tax liability for funds, *Japan* is the frontrunner in regard to the tax rate. A tax rate of approximately 42 % is charged on investment income earned by a Japanese company equity fund. At a distribution ratio of at least 90 % of the net income generated, the payouts can generally be deducted from the assessment base. When a company equity fund distributes all of the investment income, it can thus avoid income taxation.

Due to their conception following civil law, funds in the *USA* are always subject to the same tax laws as corporations. If, however, the fund meets certain requirements,[54] it qualifies as a "Regulated Investment Company" (RIC) and can then opt for a more favourable tax regime that, among other benefits, allows payouts to the investors to be deducted from the tax assessment base at fund level. Investment income of RICs is then subject to income taxation of funds only to the extent that it is retained; the tax rate applied here is 35 %. An additional indirect tax (the so-called *excise tax*) of 4 % is levied when less than 98 % of the distributable investment income is paid out to the investors. Regardless of how and to what extent their profits are used (distributed or accumulated), unregulated funds are subject to independent income taxation.

Tax law in the *United Kingdom* differentiates between funds that distribute dividends and those that distribute interest. Both have in common that they are not subject to taxation of income gained from the disposal of assets.[55] If a fund exceeds its investment quota of 60 % in interest-bearing securities within a distribution period, the fund can opt to be classified as a fund that distributes interest. If this option is not chosen, it is treated as a fund that distributes dividends. In both cases the classification has a comprehensive effect in that the fund payouts in their entirety are considered either interest or dividends. In addition to the relevance of this classification for subsequent taxation purposes (withholding tax at fund level, allocation to a specific type of income and taxation dependent thereon at investor level), it also plays an important role in the scope of the tax liability at fund level. Current income from equity securities is generally not subject to income tax liability at fund level. Interest income is treated differently: it is always taxed at a rate of 20 %. But since interest paid out to the investors is deductible at fund level from the tax assessment base, there is no regular charge of independent tax at the level of interest-paying funds either. Any capital gains are exempt from taxation at fund level and are re-invested in the fund.

---

[54] Refer to the country Chap. 3 of this study for more detailed information.

[55] The factual tax exemption on capital gains applies only in the case that fund activities do not qualify as securities trading under British law.

Based on the independent tax liability of funds, *Spain* levies a tax of 1 % on investment income at fund level. The lowest income tax rate is in the *Netherlands*, where income of funds under the FBI regime are subject to a tax of 0 %, meaning they are de facto tax exempt.

2.2.3.2 Consideration at Fund Level of Withholding Taxes Withheld at Asset Level

Domestic Case

When dealing with the independent tax liability of funds, a central issue is whether domestic withholding taxes withheld at asset level can be offset/considered when the fund level is taxed. To prevent income components of independently taxable investment funds from being subjected to multiple income-related taxes, all of the withholding taxes levied at previous levels must be taken into consideration to relieve the tax burden at fund level. However, this demand is no longer justified in cases in which the withholding tax was charged at asset level on behalf of the investor behind the fund.[56]

Table 2.5 shows the possibilities for consideration at fund level of withholding taxes withheld at asset level for domestic cases in the countries examined here. The following information is also valid for cross-border case 2 (same tax jurisdiction regarding assets and funds).

In eight of the 13 countries (*Germany, France, Ireland, Japan, Luxembourg, Poland, USA, United Kingdom*), no withholding taxes are levied at all at asset level on behalf of the creditor of the investment income in the domestic case.[57] So there is no need to examine this aspect further for these countries.

In the *Netherlands*, however, there must be differentiation between the various types of funds in regard to possible ways to take into consideration the withholding tax. Compared to the cases in other countries mentioned above, the possible considerations are basically not as comprehensive. It is only with FBIs that withholding taxation at asset level (indirect) is incorporated: the withholding tax rate at fund level, levied upon fund distribution to investors, is reduced. With funds of the VBI type, the retained withholding taxes are already reduced to 0 % at asset level, so there is no need to implement further measures at the level of the factual tax-exempt investment funds. Just like funds set up as limited partnerships in the legal form CV, funds created in the legal form FGR for the joint account of their investors are treated as transparent for tax purposes, meaning that the income from the assets is directly allocated to investors and taxed at that level. Consequentially, in such cases there is no way to consider withholding taxes levied at asset level in taxation at fund level.

---

[56] This would then lead to the systematic requirement of a possibility for consideration at investor level; for more on this, refer to Sect. 2.2.4.4.

[57] Also refer to Table 2.2.

Table 2.5 Consideration at fund level of withholding taxes withheld at asset level in the domestic case (basic case and cross-border case 2)

Country in which the fund is located		Possibilities for consideration at fund level of withholding taxes withheld at asset level				
		Refund	Offsetting and potential refund	Offsetting against withholding tax at fund level	Cannot be considered	No withholding taxes at asset level
Denmark	"Distributing fund"					X
	Investment company				X	
Germany						X
France						X
Ireland						X
Italy					X	
Japan						X
Luxembourg						X
Netherlands	FBI			X		
	VBI					X
	FGR/CV				X	
Poland						X
Switzerland		X				
Spain			X			
USA (RIC)						X
United Kingdom						X

In *Denmark* differentiation between the specific types of funds is also necessary with regard to tax treatment. While the withholding tax rate is reduced to 0 % at asset level when the creditor is a "distributing fund" investment income to which investment companies are entitled is subject to withholding taxation at the regular rate. However, this withholding tax liability cannot be considered at fund level, because investment companies are factual tax-exempt. *Italy* always denies considering any asset level withholding taxes at fund level. So the tax burden of the withholding taxes retained at asset level depends in such cases on whether consideration can occur at investor level instead.[58]

Switzerland grants a refund of the preliminarily withheld taxes to domestic investment funds that are personally tax-exempt due to their ascribed transparency for tax purposes. As independently taxable entities, funds in *Spain* can offset domestic withholding taxes already withheld from the income gained on the assets. In addition, the funds can receive a refund of the excess tax credits when the final income tax to be paid by the fund is less than the anticipated withholding tax

---
[58] Refer to section "Domestic Case" in Sect. 2.2.4.4.

2.2 Taxation of Income from Investment Funds

Table 2.6 Consideration at domestic fund level of foreign withholding taxes withheld at asset level in the international case pursuant to unilateral regulations (cross-border case 1 and three-country case)[a]

Country in which the fund is located		Offsetting	Offsetting against withholding taxes at fund level	Reduction of calculated minimum distribution	Cannot be considered
Denmark	"Distributing fund"			X	
	Investment company				X
Germany			X		
France					X
Ireland					X
Italy					X
Japan	Contract fund		X		
	Company fund	X			
Luxembourg					X
Netherlands	FGR/CV				X
	FBI		X		
	VBI				X
Poland					X
Switzerland					X
Spain		X			
USA (RIC)		X			
United Kingdom		X			

[a]Double taxation agreements can in some cases prescribe different measures to avoid double taxation

retained on behalf of the fund at asset level. The result is that applicable withholding taxes at asset level are fully offset.

International Case

Table 2.6 presents the possibilities for a fund to take into consideration the withholding taxes at asset level in compliance with the law of the fund's country of residency when the withholding taxes are paid in a different country (cross-border case 1 and three-country case).

Because foreign withholding taxes at asset level can be offset, *Japan*, *Spain*, the *USA* and the *United Kingdom* are able to ensure that taxable investment funds residing in these countries are not subject to double income taxation with their foreign proceeds.

Funds in *Germany* are exempt from income taxation just as are contract type funds in *Japan* and the de facto tax-exempt funds of the FBI type in the *Netherlands*. So there can be no offsetting because there is no base to offset against.

In such cases foreign withholding taxes at asset level are applied alternatively to the fund level taken into account by offsetting them against the withholding taxes levied at fund level. This means that the level of the investment fund, between the assets and the investor, likewise poses no greater tax burden than direct investment in the assets.

But what both variations have in common is that offsetting of foreign taxes is regularly limited to the amount of the domestic income taxes to be paid on the foreign income.

Denmark's tax law provides for a weakened form of the withholding tax consideration for "distributing funds" and allows only a deduction from the calculated minimum distribution (to be charged in turn at fund level with the compulsory domestic withholding tax).[59]

Consideration of the withholding taxes at asset level by the fund is generally denied in *France, Ireland, Italy, Luxembourg, Poland* and *Switzerland*. It also does not apply to investment companies in *Denmark* or to funds structured as VBI and FGR/CV in the *Netherlands*. Since investment funds are not subject to an independent income tax in these nine cases, the failure to consider foreign withholding taxes from the systematic point of view cannot be criticized.

In so far as withholding taxes at asset level are not claimed for funds, this likewise does not rule out that withholding taxes can be taken into consideration at the level of the investor instead. Furthermore, double taxation agreements can prescribe different measures.[60]

2.2.3.3 Offsetting Losses at Fund Level

Offsetting losses at fund level for tax purposes poses a second significant aspect of taxation of investment income: balancing positive and negative income of a fund may reduce the assessment base and thus directly reduce the tax burden. Table 2.7 shows the type and scope of existing possibilities for offsetting losses in the countries examined.

Six of the countries examined always disallow offsetting losses at fund level for tax purposes. These countries are *France, Ireland, Italy, Luxembourg, Poland* and *Switzerland*[61]. Funds of the VBI type and FGR/CV in the *Netherlands*, in *Japan* (contract type) and regulated investment companies (RIC) in the *USA* are also excluded from offsetting losses.

In six cases there are more or less restrictive possibilities to carry forward accrued tax losses from one tax year to future tax years. *Denmark, Germany* and the *United Kingdom* deal more generously with this issue, in regard to time as well

---

[59] Refer to Sect. 2.2.3.4.

[60] Refer to section "International Case" in Sect. 2.2.4.4.

[61] But in regard to Switzerland, it should be noted that denial of loss offsetting for tax purposes applies only to purposes related to income taxation of investment funds. Since funds are independently liable for withholding tax purposes, in this respect intratemporal loss compensation is granted; refer to the Eidgenössische Steuerverwaltung (2009), p. 21 et seq.

2.2 Taxation of Income from Investment Funds

Table 2.7 Offsetting losses for tax purposes at fund level in the domestic case

Country in which the fund is located		Time dimension of fund loss offsetting			Fund losses cannot be offset
		Loss carry-forward		Loss carry-back	
		No limitation	Time limitation		
Denmark		X			
Germany		X			
France					X
Ireland					X
Italy					X
Japan	Company type		7 years		
	Contract type				X
Luxembourg					X
Netherlands	FBI		9 years	1 year	
	FGR/CV, VBI				X
Poland					X
Switzerland					X
Spain			15 years		
USA (RIC)					X
United Kingdom		X		Time depends on individual case	

as to amounts. There are time restrictions governing the capacity to carry forward losses in three cases. In *Japan* the time limit is 7 years for funds of the company type. Tax law in the *Netherlands* applies the same regulations to loss offsetting for funds of the FBI type as generally apply to corporations; this means that loss carry-forward is limited to 9 years. In *Spain* losses carried forward expire after 15 years.

Loss carry-back, meaning the possibility of offsetting losses against profits from previous years, can be applied in two cases. In the *Netherlands* FBI can carry back losses to the preceding year. In the *United Kingdom* there is no restriction on the amount of losses that can be carried back. The time limit for carry-back depends on the specific case though and is a factor of the specific type of income that the loss can be attributed to.

2.2.3.4 Withholding Taxation of Investors at Fund Level
Domestic Case

The tax systems of the 13 countries have already been analysed in regard to the aspect of independent income tax liability of investment funds and in regard to whether retained domestic withholding taxes at asset level can be claimed for the fund itself. This section will offer insight regarding the countries that levy domestic withholding taxes at fund level on the account of the investors and the countries that potentially allow a delay of taxation at investor level through accumulation at fund level. Based on the type and scope of withholding taxation on behalf of the investor, there is once again differentiation between the domestic case or the cross-border case 1 (treated the same in this respect) and the cross-border case 2.

Table 2.8 Obligation to distribute the income earned to the investors in the domestic case (basic case and cross-border case 1)

Country in which the fund is located		Distribution obligation for taxation reasons	
		Yes	No
Denmark	"Distributing fund"		X
	Investment company		X
Germany			X
France			X
Ireland			X
Italy			X
Japan			X
Luxembourg			X
Netherlands	FBI	X	
	FGR/CV, VBI		X
Poland			X
Switzerland			X
Spain			X
USA (RIC)		X	
United Kingdom		X	

In three of the cases examined, for investment funds there is always a taxation-related obligation to distribute the investment income earned to the investors (refer to Table 2.8); consequently, taxation of the investor cannot be deferred in these cases.

In the *Netherlands*, FBIs are subject to mandatory distribution within 8 months of the end of the tax year. If the FBI shows a positive balance due to taxable profits and losses from the disposal of assets, the surplus can be allocated to a tax-exempt reserve for re-investment and taxable income reduced, so only the remaining taxable income is subject to mandatory distribution (which is liable to withholding tax) to the investors. In addition to realised capital gains, this option is also available for all unrealised capital gains; ordinary dividend and interest income, on the other hand, cannot be allocated to the reserve for re-investment. In the *USA*, RICs are obligated to distribute at least 90 % of the taxable interest and dividend income; hence realised capital gains are not subject to compulsory distribution. Finally, tax law of the *United Kingdom* dictates that all net income earned in a year be distributed; portions that are actually accumulated are considered for tax purposes to be distributed to investors.

Although there is no compulsory distribution for investment funds in *Denmark*, "distributing funds" must calculate a fictitious minimum distribution which is still subject to the full withholding tax.

For final consideration of the tax consequences at fund level, it must still be determined to what extent the investors behind the funds are subject to preliminary levying of withholding taxes at fund level in the countries examined. Table 2.9 offers insight into the context of the domestic case. When withholding taxation at

2.2 Taxation of Income from Investment Funds

Table 2.9 Withholding tax deduction at fund level on behalf of the investor in the domestic case (basic case and cross-border case 1)

Country in which the fund is located		Withholding tax — Not until distribution by fund	Withholding tax — Independent of appropriation of earnings at fund level	No withholding tax
Denmark	Distributing bond funds			X
	Other distributing funds		28 %	
	Investment companies			X
Germany	Dividends, interest		26.375 %	
	Capital gains	26.375 %		
France	Right to choose PFL — Exercised	30.1 %		
	Not exercised			X
Ireland	Dividends, interest	25 %		
	Capital gains	28 %		
Italy	Dividends, interest, capital gains	20 %		
	Government bonds and similar securities	12.5 %		
Japan	Bond funds of the contract type	20 %		
	Other funds	10 %		
Luxembourg				X
Netherlands	FBI — Dividends	15 %		
	Interest, capital gains			X
	VBI, FGR/CV			X
Poland		19 %		
Switzerland	Distributing funds — Dividends, interest	35 %		
	Capital gains (separate coupon)			X
	Mixed or cumulative funds — Dividends, interest		35 %	
	Capital gains (separate coupon)			X
Spain		19 %		
USA (RIC)				X
United Kingdom	(Fictitious) dividends		10 %	
	(Fictitious) interest		20 %	

fund level and withholding taxation at asset level are compared (refer to Sect. 2.2.2), it is obvious that the countries examined are attempting to apply taxation less at the interface between investment object and fund, and more at the interface between the fund and the investor. Nine of the 13 countries completely refrain in the domestic case from deducting tax at asset level, while only three of the 13 countries levy no withholding tax at all at fund level.

Tables 2.8 and 2.9 indicate that investors in the *United Kingdom* and in the *Netherlands* who invest in an FBI are subject to a withholding tax at fund level that cannot be significantly deferred. Tax law in the United Kingdom stipulates a 20 % withholding tax on distributed interest income or interest income that is treated as distributed, while respective dividend income is subject to only 10 % withholding tax. It should be borne in mind in this context that fund distributions are considered in their entirety to be interest when more than 60 % of the fund assets are invested in interest-bearing investment objects and the fund therefore elects to make interest distributions. When the investment quota is lower, distributions are considered to be dividends. In the case of Dutch FBIs, the withholding tax rate is 15 %. In addition, withholding taxes deducted at asset level take effect here. The deduction is effected by reducing the withholding tax levied on the FBI's distributions to its investors by the domestic withholding tax rate at asset level.

Regardless of the existence or lack of explicit compulsory distribution, two other countries levy withholding taxes at fund level on behalf of the investor in the domestic case, without taking into consideration the fund's profit utilization (distribution or retention). In *Denmark* investors engaged in "distributing funds" are subject to a 28 % withholding tax. The withholding tax deduction is waived in the exceptional case of a "distributing fund" that invests only in bonds. Withholding taxes are also waived in the case of participation in investment companies. In *Switzerland* a withholding tax of 35 % is levied in the case of mixed or cumulative funds, regardless of the use of earnings at fund level. However, profit from the disposal of assets is generally exempt from taxation at fund level, if it can be reported or distributed separately from the current income earned on equity securities and bonds. If this couponing (separation) is not applied though, capital gains are also subject to the withholding tax that is levied regardless of whether earnings are paid out to the investors or accumulated in the fund. Investors engaged in distributing funds are not liable to tax until distribution. In order for a fund to qualify as distributing fund it must distribute at least 70 % of its income. A fund with a distribution quota of less than 70 % is designated a mixed fund. Funds are referred to as cumulative funds only if they are fully non-distributing.

Germany differentiates between ordinary and extraordinary income. To the extent that current income from equity securities and bonds is affected, the fund investors are subject to a withholding tax of 26.375 % at fund level, regardless of whether earnings are actually distributed. Capital gains generated by the fund can take advantage of an accumulation privilege: such gains are taxed at the same rate, but not until the time of distribution.

Deferment of the withholding tax deduction at fund level through accumulation of the income at fund level is firstly conceivable in *Ireland*. The tax is not deducted

2.2 Taxation of Income from Investment Funds

in this country until the investment income is transferred to the investors, the rate being 25 % on dividends and interest and 28 % on capital gains. *Italy* always levies withholding tax, unrelated to the type of income, at a harmonized rate of 20 %. But when the transferred income is from fund investments in government bonds and comparable securities, only 12.5 % is withheld at the time of distribution. In *Japan* the withholding tax rate at fund level is a factor of the fund type and of the composition of the fund portfolio: while investment funds of the contract type that invest exclusively in bonds must retain a withholding tax of 20 % on behalf of the investors at the time of distribution, a reduced tax rate of 10 % is applied to funds with a mixed asset portfolio; the latter quoted tax rate applies regardless of the asset portfolio also for all other types of fund. *Poland* and *Spain* both levy a 19 % withholding tax.

Withholding tax at fund level is waived in *France*, *Luxembourg* and the *USA*. *France*, however, allows resident investors to choose between final taxation at fund level with the so-called *prélèvement forfaitaire libératoire* (PFL) of 30.1 %[62] and the assessment of the income from the fund to income tax[63], whereby there is no withholding tax at all with the latter option.

International Case

If the investor resides in a different country than that in which the fund is located (cross-border case 2 and three-country case), the aspect of limited tax liability of the investor becomes relevant. Withholding tax that is potentially deducted at fund level serves to ensure that income earned in the source country (in this case, the location of the fund) is taxed in that country. Table 2.10 shows which countries levy withholding tax at fund level when the investor resides in a different country.

The withholding tax rate in the international case is a factor of requirements that differ substantially amongst the countries, both on the merits and in terms of amount. It can even differ within a single country, depending on the type of fund and income in the individual case. *Poland* (19 %), *Spain* (19 %) and the *USA* (30 %) are the only countries that apply undifferentiated tax rates.

As in the domestic case, *Denmark* deducts no withholding tax on behalf of the investor when the fund invests exclusively in bonds. Unilaterally, the withholding tax rate of 28 % that applies to the domestic case can be reduced when the foreign investor resides in a qualified country, is registered with the proper authorities in Denmark, has a Danish bank account, and provides Danish authorities with information on his domicile.

Germany refrains from charging foreign investors withholding tax at fund level when the current investment income is earned on bonds or from capital gains generated by the fund. On the other hand, the fund must levy withholding tax of 26.375 %, as in the domestic case when German dividend income is transferred to a foreign investor.

---

[62] Combined tax rate of 18 % original withholding tax and 12.1 % social contributions.

[63] Refer to Sect. 2.2.4 for more information.

Table 2.10 Withholding tax deduction at fund level on behalf of the investor in the international case pursuant to unilateral regulations (cross-border case 2 and three-country case)[a]

Country in which the fund is located				Withholding tax	No withholding tax
Denmark	Bond funds				X
	Other funds			28 %	
Germany	Dividends			26.375 %	
	Interest, capital gains				X
France	FCP	Domestic assets	Dividends	25 %	
			Interest	15 %	
		Foreign assets			X
	SICAV	Solely domestic bonds			X
		Other funds	Qualified investor	18 %	
			Other investors	25 %	
Ireland	With proof of "foreign investor"				X
	No proof of "foreign investor"	Dividends, interest		25 %	
		Capital gains		28 %	
Italy	Investor from "white list country"				X
	Other investors	Dividends, interest, capital gains		20 %	
		Government bonds and similar securities		12.5 %	
Japan	Contract type	Bond funds		15 %	
		Other funds		7 %	
	Company type	Bond funds		7 %	
		Other funds		7 %	
Luxembourg	Dividends, capital gains				X
	Interest	EU investor		20 %	
		Non-EU investor			X
Netherlands	FBI	Dividends		15 %	
		Interest, capital gains			
	VBI, FGR/CV				X
Poland				19 %	
Switzerland	Requirements for affidavit process	Fulfilled			X
		Not fulfilled		35 %	
Spain				19 %	
USA (RIC)				30 %	
United Kingdom	Dividends (fictitious)				X
	Interest (ficticious)	With proof of "foreign investor"			X
		Without proof of "foreign investor"		20 %	

[a]In some cases double taxation agreements may prescribe lower tax rates

2.2 Taxation of Income from Investment Funds

While *France* refrains in the domestic case from withholding tax at fund level, it is only in exceptional cases that no withholding tax is levied in the international case. Since an FCP is transparent for tax purposes, no tax is withheld at fund level when income from assets located in foreign countries is distributed to foreign investors. Income from domestic equity securities, on the other hand, is subject to 25 % withholding tax at this level, while income from domestic bonds is subject to a reduced rate of 15 %. In regard to SICAV, the composition of the investment portfolio is relevant to begin with: the obligation to deduct withholding tax is waived only for investments in bonds located exclusively in one's own country. The amount of withholding tax to be charged to other SICAV is a factor of whether the investors are "qualified" through residency in another EU member country, in Iceland or in Norway. If this is the case, the regular rate of 25 % is reduced to 18 % pursuant to unilateral law. If a SICAV distributes capital gains, the foreign investor is liable for withholding tax on this income only if there was a minimum shareholding amount of 25 % without interruption over the last 5 years before distribution of the capital gains.

When the investor provides proof of foreign residency, *Ireland* exempts fund distributions from withholding tax. If the claim of foreign residency is not plausible, transferred income from equity securities and interest-bearing securities is subject to 25 % withholding tax and distributed capital gains to 28 %.

Italy exempts distributions to foreign investors from withholding tax when the country of residency of the investor maintains an appropriate exchange of information with Italy ("white list country"). Distributions to investors who are not qualified are subject to a withholding tax rate of 20 %. A reduced rate of 12.5 % is again applied to income earned on government bonds and similar interest-bearing securities.

In *Japan* a withholding tax of 7 % is always levied at fund level on the distribution of investment income to foreign investors; in the case of bond funds created as contract type funds, a higher rate of 15 % applies.

Luxembourg always exempts fund distributions to foreign countries from tax liability. But one exception exists in the case of interest income transferred to a different EU member country, which is subject to a 20 % withholding tax as a result of the EU interest information decree.[64]

In the *Netherlands*, only the transfer by FBI of income from equity securities is subject to a 15 % withholding tax at fund level. Interest and capital gains through FBI can be transferred free of withholding tax. Investors from across borders with units in VBI or FGR/CV always receive distributions gross.

Switzerland treats the international case basically the same as the domestic case when it comes to withholding tax at fund level. But the 35 % withholding tax can be

---

[64] Pursuant to the EU CD (2003/48/EC), Luxembourg is, for a transition period, exempted from the obligation to automatically provide information to the investor's country of location; however, withholding tax must be levied instead.

avoided when the requirements are met for the so-called affidavit process. To meet the requirements, an investor residing outside of Switzerland must have invested in investment funds located in Switzerland, the depository bank must confirm foreign residency, and the fund must earn at least 80 % of its income from assets located outside of Switzerland. If such a three-country case exists, the income can be distributed gross to the investor.

In the *United Kingdom* the differentiation between dividend and interest distribution, a factor of the classification of the investment fund as a bond fund or other fund, is significant: while distributions considered dividends are not subject to withholding tax, gross distribution of income considered interest can occur only when it can be plausibly proven to the tax authorities that the investor is not a resident of the United Kingdom. Otherwise withholding tax of 26 % is levied, as in the domestic case.

2.2.3.5 Preliminary Conclusions on Taxation at Fund Level

It is already apparent even when observation is reduced to the *domestic case* that none of the 13 countries examined completely eliminates the investment fund level for tax purposes. The identified violations of this clearly defined and comprehended understanding of transparent taxation are of varying severity and include essentially:

- Tax deductions at asset level for certain types of funds or income that is of a temporary nature because it can be refunded or offset (Netherlands, Switzerland, Spain) or also of a definitive nature (Denmark, Italy)
- Levying of (even though they are low) subscription taxes (Luxembourg)
- Clearly specified subject tax liabilities of investment funds themselves, but of differing scope (Germany, Japan, Spain, USA, United Kingdom)
- Regulations that influence the assessment base, regarding offsetting of losses at fund level (Denmark, Germany, Japan, Netherlands, Spain, United Kingdom)
- Tax-related intervention in decisions on the profit utilization (distribution or retention) at fund level (Netherlands, USA, United Kingdom)
- Tax deductions at fund level on behalf of the investors, that potentially could apply independently of whether the income accrued to the fund is actually paid out to the investors (Denmark, Germany, Switzerland, United Kingdom), or tax deductions that can be deferred through accumulation at fund level (France, Ireland, Italy, Japan, Netherlands, Poland, Spain).

If the investor in the fund does not reside in the country in which the fund is located, there are different taxation consequences at fund level that apply. Unlike the domestic case, in the *international case* withholding taxation at fund level is intended to secure the tax base in the country in which the fund is located, the so-called source country. This goes along with highly heterogeneous regulation structures between as well as within the countries examined. Potentially existing double taxation agreements may increase complexity: they generally specify a reduction of the domestic withholding tax to 10–15 %.

2.2.4 Consequences of Taxation at Investor Level

2.2.4.1 Time That Tax Liability Is Incurred in the Domestic Case

In the countries examined, various criteria determine whether and, if so, when an investor incurs a tax liability in regard to the investment income from the fund. In addition to the type of fund, decisive factors in this issue can be on the one hand the type and scope of profit utilization (distribution or retention) at fund level, and on the other hand the specific composition of the fund participation, as well as the allocation of fund units to personal or business assets of the investor. Also, there are cases in which the treasuries do not target the income actually earned but instead use divergent tax bases or even assumptions about the distribution behaviour of the fund as a basis. Table 2.11 clearly shows the heterogeneity related to the facts which create the investor's tax liability.

Investors with units in "distributing funds" in *Denmark* are subject to a flat personal tax rate of 28 % or 42 % on income from equity securities (*share income*). The tax rate is a factor of their taxable income. In contrast, a progressive tax rate is applied to income from bonds; the marginal tax rate on this *capital income* can be as high as 52 %. If a Danish "distributing fund" does not pass on distributable investment income to investors, the purchase price of the investors' fund units rises. In the case of investment companies, investors are confronted with a special tax regime: it is not only the distributed dividends, interest or capital gains, but also the appreciation of the capital invested in the fund that is subject to taxation. Regardless of whether the income is distributed or retained, all these items are taxed *as capital income* at a rate of up to 52 %.

As to the time at which the tax liability arises for an investor in *Germany*, it is decisive whether current investment income is at issue or investment income that the fund earned through disposal of assets. While the latter investment income is not taxable until distribution at investor level, taxation is not a factor of profit utilization for current income. It must also be differentiated between fund units held by the investor as personal assets or as business assets. When units are included in personal assets, a flat rate tax is applied, whereby the investor's tax liability is always satisfied conclusively with the deduction of withholding tax at fund level.[65] But if the units are part of the business assets, the investment income must be reported by the investor for income tax assessment purposes. Then only 60 % of income from equity securities is taxed at the personal progressive income tax rate of 14–45 % (plus 5.5 % solidarity surcharge thereon). 100 % of income from bonds is included in the assessment base for income tax. In addition, trade tax is due on this income in the case that the units are held as business assets.

In *France*, investors can choose between assessment of 60 % of the distributions considered dividends or 100 % of the distribution considered interest with the four step income tax rate (5.5 %, 14 %, 30 %, and 40 %) and flat rate taxation at fund

---

[65] If assessment at the personal progressive tax rate would be more beneficial to the investor, he may petition to apply the assessment instead of flat rate taxation.

Table 2.11 Impact of profit appropriation policy at fund level on the tax liability of the investor (basic case and cross-border case 1)

Country in which the investor is located		Incursion of investor's tax liability				
		Dividends/interest		Capital gains		
		Not until distribution by fund	Independent of appropriation of earnings at fund level	Not until distribution by fund	Independent of appropriation of earnings at fund level	Fictitious, calculatory assessment base (independent of appropriation of earnings at fund level)
Denmark	Distributing funds	X		X		
	Investment company	X		X		X
Germany			X	X		
France		X		X		
Ireland		n/a		n/a		
Italy	Business assets	X		X		
	Personal assets	n/a		n/a		
Japan		n/a		n/a		
Luxembourg	FCP		X		X	
	SICAV	X		X		
Netherlands						X
Poland		n/a		n/a		
Switzerland	Distributing funds	X		X		
	Mixed or cumulative funds (private assets)		X		X[a]	
	Mixed or cumulative funds (business assets)	X		X		
Spain		X		X		
USA (RIC)		X			X	
United Kingdom			X	n/a		

[a] When units are held in personal assets, the investor has no tax liability on capital gains earned by the fund when the gains are reported separately or distributed with a separate coupon

2.2 Taxation of Income from Investment Funds

level of 100 % of the gross amount of distributions, with a proportional tax rate of 30.1 %.[66] Accumulated earnings generally do not accrue to the investor. However, an exception applies to natural persons holding more than 10 % in FCP. In these cases capital gains realized by the fund are subject to income tax at the level of the investor irrespective of whether the capital gains are distributed or retained.

Besides taxation at fund level as shown in Table 2.9, *Ireland* levies no other taxes at investor level. The same applies in principle to *Japan* unless the investor files a tax return thus opting for income taxation at investor level (rather than for final taxation at fund level).

Italy's tax law differentiates between whether an investor holds his fund units as personal or business assets. In the first case, the investor's tax liability is fulfilled with the 20 % or 12.5 % withholding tax at fund level, and there is no additional taxation at investor level. When units are business assets though, 49.72 % of the distributed investment income (partial income procedure) must be subjected by the investor to the progressive income tax, the rate of which ranges from 23 % to 43 %.

Investors in *Luxembourg* are subject to progressive income tax rates between 0 % and 38.95 %. Units in an FCP incur income tax liability in which appropriation of earnings is irrelevant, while investors have to pay tax on investment income from shares in an SICAV only when they actually receive such income through distribution.

Similar to taxation of the investors in investment companies in Denmark, investors in the *Netherlands* are subject to income tax liability, in which appropriation of earnings is irrelevant, founded on a calculatory assessment base. This means that 4 % of the average market value of the fund portfolio is taxed at a proportional rate of 30 %.

The income tax liability of investors in *Poland* is taken care of with the withholding tax of 19 % at fund level; thus there is no additional taxation at investor level.

Tax law in *Switzerland* specifies the time of incursion of a personal tax liability by a domestic investor to be on the one hand a question of whether or not the investor holds units in a distribution fund. On the other hand, it may in individual cases be relevant whether the fund units are held as private or business assets. An investment fund qualifies as a distribution fund when it transfers at least 70 % of its distributable income to the investors. The investors are then only liable for tax on the distributed income. Furthermore, distributions from capital gains can be tax-exempt at investor level when they are distributed with a separate coupon and the fund units are held as part of the investor's personal assets. If the distribution quota of the fund is below 70 % (mixed and cumulative funds), pass-through taxation is applied in the event that the fund units are held as private assets and the total fund income (with the exception of any capital gains distributed with a separate coupon) is subject to taxation at investor level, appropriation of earnings being irrelevant. In principle, where fund units are held as business assets, income is not subject to

---

[66] Refer to section "Domestic Case" in Sect. 2.2.3.4.

taxation until the time of distribution. The applicable tax rate is comprised of two components: the federal tax with tax rates between 0 % and 11.5 % and an annex tax owed to the canton, the rate of which varies by canton.

Spain levies a proportional 19 % income tax on distributions paid by the fund at investor level as savings income.

In the *USA* private investors with shares in a regulated investment company (RIC) are subject to an income tax rate between 10 % and 35 % on the distributed dividends (These include profits from the fund's disposal of short-term assets) and interest. Capital gains arising on the sale of long-term assets (held for longer than 12 months) are subject to tax at investor level at personal income tax rates ranging between 0 % and 15 % irrespective of whether or not the income is distributed.

Depending on qualification of the fund as bond fund or non-bond fund, investors residing in the *United Kingdom* receive either interest income or dividend income; any capital gains from the fund's disposal of assets are re-invested in the fund and are hence irrelevant for income tax purposes. Depending on the amount, dividend income is subject to tax rates of 10 %, 32.5 %, or 42.5 %, while the tax rates applying to interest income are 10 %, 20 %, 40 %, and 50 %.

2.2.4.2 Consequences for the "Transparency" of Taxation in Regard to the Investor
Domestic Case

The question of which profit appropriation policy at fund level has which consequences for taxation at investor level, can be asked in a systematically consistent tax system only when fund taxation is not to be considered transparent. If the principle of transparency is to apply, the fund level must have no significance for tax purposes; the investment income earned from the assets would be directly attributable to the investor and taxable only at this level.

In *Denmark* the appropriation of earnings is irrelevant only in regard to investors with shares in investment companies. If the investor holds units in a "distributing fund", there is no independent tax liability of the investor until actual distribution of the investment income. At the same time, appropriation of earnings is irrelevant with regard to the withholding tax which is levied at fund level on behalf of the investor, unless the "distributing fund" invests exclusively in bonds. Inasmuch as the time of withholding tax deduction at fund level and its consideration for income taxation purposes at investor level differ, the investor is subject to negative interest effects. The financial losses resulting from deferment of the withholding tax claim increase as more time passes until the prior tax burden is offset with the final income tax liability.

In the remaining cases examined in the study, no indications for the occurrence of negative time and interest effects can be identified. However, the investment taxation terms exhibit other weaknesses related to the tax system in three cases.

Table 2.4 categorised fund types according to the question of whether or not they are taxable entities. According to this, French FCP, Dutch FGR/CV and the funds in Switzerland included in the study are not taxable entities. It must be ensured that investors cannot gain deferment of income taxation with the intermediation of a fund. The *Netherlands* actually take this into account by applying, as shown, investor taxation on a mark-to-market basis. In *France*, on the other hand, incursion of income tax liability at investor level requires distribution of the investment income earned by incursion of fund. *Switzerland* applies the same principle to cases in which the fund distributes at least 70 % of the income earned in a tax year to the investors. Accordingly, transparent taxation of the investment income is in principle only achieved when the fund distributes less than 70 % of income.

International Case
In cross-border case 2 and the three-country case, the investor resides in a different country than the fund. Because of this, regulations in regard to the investor's independent tax liability that differ from the domestic case apply in some countries. Tax law in *Ireland* differentiates between three types of foreign investment funds. Special tax rates are applied, depending on the legal form of the foreign fund in which the domestic investor invests. When units are held in regulated funds in EU or OECD countries with which Ireland has signed a double taxation agreement, taxes are levied as in the domestic case. This means that dividends and interest are subject to a tax rate of 26 %, while capital gains are taxed at 28 %. If the fund is not regulated, dividends and interest are subject to the individual marginal income tax rate of the investor, while capital gains are taxed at 25 %. In all other cases, all income from the fund investment is subject to the individual marginal tax rate. *Italian* investors in funds located in countries that belong to the EU or the EEA and that ensure adequate exchange of information receive the same tax treatment as in the domestic case. When the fund is located in a country that does not meet these requirements, income is assessed at investor level. In some cases in *Japan*, it can occur that the local Controlled Foreign Company rules dictate that the investor be taxed on the income accumulated at fund level in a different country. Comparable regulations apply in the *USA*: three different taxation systems are possible for investors residing in the USA, with shares in passive foreign investment companies.[67]

2.2.4.3 Relevance of Income Qualification at Investor Level
If a country's tax law ascribes taxation-related relevance to the fund level, consideration of the fund as a relevant participant may lead to consequences for further treatment of the original investment income at investor level. Particularly in countries that differentiate between various types of income, the allocation of income earned from the fund, which occurs at investor level, to these types of income influences the type and scope of income taxation. Thus the following analysis looks at whether an investor's income from his investment retains its original nature or whether tax law may effect a divergent qualification of this income. Table 2.12 shows that, in regard to the cases examined, income is mostly assigned a qualification that differs from its original nature, meaning that, for

---
[67] Detailed information on this topic can be found in the country Chap. 3 of this study.

Table 2.12 Determinants of income qualification at investor level

Country in which the investor is located			Income qualification at investor level	
			Retention of original nature of income	Disregard of original nature of income
Denmark	"Distributing fund"		X	
	Investment company			X
Germany				X
France	FCP		X	
	SICAV	Separate coupons	X	
		No separate coupons		X
Ireland				X
Italy				X
Japan				X
Luxembourg	FCP		X	
	SICAV			X
Netherlands				X
Poland				X
Switzerland	Personal assets		X	
	Business assets			X
Spain				X
USA (RIC)				X
United Kingdom				X

income tax purposes of the investor, the income qualification occurs divergently from the original and actually existing assets.

In a third of the cases examined here, intermediation of a fund does not effect any changes to the allocation of income influencing tax burden.

In regard to investment income distributed to investors from "distributing funds" in *Denmark*, qualification as *share income* applies when there is (ordinary or extraordinary) income from equity securities. In contrast to this, distributions from interest income or profit from the disposal of bonds is considered *capital income* for the investor. To be able to maintain the nature of the income for shares in a SICAV in *France*, separate coupons must be formed at fund level for the different types of income; in contrast, income earned by an FCP is always assessed as its original nature at investor level. In *Luxembourg* shareholdings in an FCP also justify maintaining the nature of the income for income tax purposes. Tax law in *Switzerland* specifies that the original nature of the income is not disregarded when the fund units are part of the investor's personal assets.

The original nature of the investment income is affected in all other cases. The consequences in the various countries are vastly different, ranging from income-type-dependent differentiation of the tax rates to modifications of the scope of the income taxation assessment base and even subsuming taxation of income that was originally different under independent tax regimes.

Investment companies in *Denmark* do not normally distribute investment income to the investors. When in exceptional cases distributions do occur, the distributed income is then treated in its entirety as *capital income* of the investor.

2.2 Taxation of Income from Investment Funds

The source of the income is ignored, as a calculatory assessment base is applied. This is particularly significant for income earned on equity securities, because in this respect the special rate for *share income* no longer applies. At investor level, investment tax law in *Germany* treats all income from fund units as income from capital regardless of its origin and nature. In *France*, without explicit coupon formation (separation), investment income of a SICAV originating from bonds is considered dividends at investor level, the consequence being that—unless the investor did not opt for flat-rate taxation at fund level—this investment income is only partially (60 %) subject to the progressive income tax rate. In the *Netherlands* investors are subject to a tax liability based on the average market value of the assets held by the fund; the origin of the income is irrelevant. In the *United Kingdom* it is significant for income qualification at investor level whether the income in question is from an investment in a fund that distributes interest or one that distributes dividends[68]; in the first case interest income is taxable, otherwise the tax arises on dividend income (at a different rate).

The withholding tax deduction at fund level[69] has a final effect in Ireland and Japan as well as on fund units held as personal assets in Italy. In *Ireland* different tax rates are applied to ordinary income from funds on the one hand and extraordinary income on the other; there is, however, no differentiation between income that formerly originated from bonds and equity securities. *Italy* maintains tax advantages at fund level for income from specific bonds; in all other cases a proportional rate applies. *Japan* applies different tax rates to distributions from bond funds than it does to all other funds. When a fund is qualified as a non-bond fund, all of its income is subject to final taxation as dividends at fund level on behalf of the investor. So interest income included partially in the distribution is also taxed at the lower rate in these cases.

There are four cases in which investment income is treated uniformly at investor level and differently than the original nature. In *Luxembourg* distributions from a SICAV are generally considered dividends for income tax purposes, regardless of their origin. In *Spain* the tax law qualifies investment income attributable to the investor as "distributions from funds", regardless of whether current investment income from bonds or equity securities or capital gains are included; the same applies in *Switzerland* in regard to fund units that are business assets. *Poland* charges a uniform tax rate at fund level, regardless of the type of income.

Investments in funds without legal capacity must not, from a systematic point of view, lead to such distortion that, at investor level, there is divergence from the income nature of the investment income. Four cases in this study lack taxable entity status.[70] The procedure applied in *France* in regard to income taxation of investors in an FCP poses no cause for criticism in this context. *Switzerland* can be accused from the systematic point of view, at least for shares held as part of business assets,

---

[68] Refer to Sect. 2.2.3 for the classification requirements.
[69] Refer to section "Domestic Case" in Sect. 2.2.3.4.
[70] Refer to Table 2.4.

Table 2.13 Consideration at investor level of domestic withholding taxes withheld at asset level in the domestic case

Country in which the investor is located		Possibilities for consideration at investor level of domestic withholding taxes withheld at asset level			
		Offsetting	Indirect deduction in the course of determining the market value oriented assessment base	Cannot be considered	No withholding tax at asset level
Denmark	"Distributing fund"				X
	Investment company		X		
Germany					X
France					X
Ireland					X
Italy				X	
Japan					X
Luxembourg					X
Netherlands	FBI			X	
	VBI				X
	FGR/CV	X			
Poland					X
Switzerland				X	
Spain				X	
USA (RIC)					X
United Kingdom					X

of violating the postulate of unmodified "transmission" of income through the fund. The same holds true for participations in contract type funds in *Japan*. Moreover, the procedure applied in the *Netherlands* of taking as an assessment base average market values at investor level also for funds of the legal form FGR/CV is not consistent with this requirement.

2.2.4.4 Consideration of Withholding Taxes from Previous Taxation Levels

Domestic Case

The following table shows the possibilities that the investor has to claim domestic withholding tax retained at previous taxation levels for income tax assessment purposes. Table 2.13 starts by showing the ways in which withholding taxes, levied at asset level in six of the 16 cases to be differentiated here, can be claimed in the domestic case.

Withholding taxes are levied at asset level in only six of the cases examined here. Consideration by the investor is granted in only two cases however. The *Netherlands* allow the investor to offset the withholding tax against his/her income tax when the investment is made via funds with the legal form FGR/CV. This regulation is proper in regard to the tax system, because the principle of transparency is strictly

2.2 Taxation of Income from Investment Funds

Table 2.14 Consideration at investor level of domestic withholding taxes withheld at fund level in the domestic case (basic case and cross-border case 1)

Country in which the investor is located		Possibilities for consideration at investor level of domestic withholding taxes withheld at fund level		
		Offsetting and potential refund	Cannot be considered	No withholding tax at fund level
Denmark	Distributing bond funds			X
	Other distributing funds	X		
	Investment companies			X
Germany	Personal assets		X	
	Business assets	X		
France				X
Ireland		X		
Italy	Personal assets		X	
	Business assets	X		
Japan		X		
Luxembourg				X
Netherlands	FBI	X		
	VBI, FGR/CV			X
Poland			X	
Switzerland[a]		X		
Spain		X		
USA (RIC)				X
United Kingdom		X		

[a] A prerequisite is that the investor is in fact taxed on the income; the specific form of the claim (offsetting and then refund of excess tax or direct refund) depends on the canton

implemented in this case. The consistent transparency of the fund level for tax purposes results in only the investor level being relevant for consideration of withholding taxes withheld at asset level.[71] Also, for collective investment in investment companies in *Denmark*, at least a deduction of withholding taxes can be applied in the course of determining the income tax assessment base, attenuating the double income tax burden. Thus the fact is taken into account that accrued withholding taxes at asset level cannot be claimed by the investment company itself.[72]

In contrast, the claim is denied in *Italy*, *Switzerland*, *Spain* and for an investment in an FBI in the *Netherlands*. There are no objections to the last three cases mentioned, because the fund can express a claim.[73] This does not apply to *Italy*; the withholding tax obligation at asset level becomes definitive there.

The possibilities for the investor to claim withholding taxes withheld at fund level are a great deal more comprehensive, as shown in Table 2.14.

---

[71] Also refer to Table 2.5, 2.9 and 2.10.
[72] Refer to Table 2.5.
[73] Ibidem.

Table 2.15 Consideration at investor level of foreign withholding taxes withheld at asset level in the international case pursuant to unilateral regulations (cross-border case 1 and three-country case)[a]

Country in which the investor is located	Possibilities for consideration at investor level of withholding taxes withheld at asset level	
	Consideration possible in individual cases	Can never be considered
Denmark	X	
Germany	X	
France		X
Ireland	X	
Italy		X
Japan	X	
Luxembourg	X	
Netherlands	X	
Poland	X	
Switzerland		X
Spain	X	
USA (RIC)	X	
United Kingdom	X	

[a]In some cases double taxation agreements may prescribe different arrangements

In 12 of the 15 cases to be differentiated, withholding tax is charged at fund level. Consideration of this charge is ensured through the investor's offsetting claims in *Denmark*, *Ireland*, *Japan*, *Switzerland*, *Spain*, the *United Kingdom*; with fund units held as business assets in *Germany* and *Italy*; and with units in an FBI in the *Netherlands*. When excess tax is withheld in the course of tax deduction, the investor regularly receives a refund.

There is no consideration in three cases, namely in *Germany* and *Italy* when the fund units are held as personal assets as well as in *Poland*. The basis for this is that the investor does not have to assess his investment income for income tax purposes in these cases. The income tax liability is met with the tax deduction at fund level.

International Case

Table 2.15 shows the extent to which the foreign withholding taxes retained at asset level can be considered at investor level, when *cross-border case 1* or the in this respect comparable *three-country case* applies, meaning that the assets are located outside of the country in which the investor is located.

It must be pointed out as an introductory note that this aspect always has to be specifically examined for the respective case. At all events, the prerequisite for claiming the foreign withholding tax is that the fund (possibly located in a foreign country) is considered by the country in which the taxable investor is located to be a transparent vehicle for tax purposes. If transparency is confirmed, ten of the 13 countries examined at least do not rule out consideration. Only France, Italy and Switzerland always rule out consideration as part of income tax assessment.

2.2 Taxation of Income from Investment Funds

Table 2.16 Consideration at investor level of foreign withholding taxes withheld at fund level in the international case pursuant to unilateral regulations (cross-border case 2 and three-country case)[a]

Country in which the investor is located	Possibilities for consideration at investor level of foreign withholding taxes withheld at fund level		
	Offsetting	Deduction	No consideration
Denmark	X		
Germany	X	X	
France			X
Ireland	X	X	
Italy			X
Japan	X		
Luxembourg[b]	X		
Netherlands	X		
Poland	X		
Switzerland			X
Spain	X		
USA	X		
United Kingdom	X	X	

[a]Double taxation agreements can in some cases prescribe different measures to avoid double taxation

[b]Offsetting takes place within the so-called half-dividend system, a type of half-income system (fundamental requirement: the country in which the fund is located is either covered by the EU parent-subsidiary directive or is a DTA partner country of the country in which the investor is located)

In conclusion of the examination of the relevant tax issues at investor level, it remains to be clarified to which extent foreign withholding taxes retained at fund level can be considered at investor level, when *cross-border case 2* or the virtually comparable *three-country case* applies, meaning that the fund is located outside of the country in which the investor is located. This is shown in Table 2.16.

The unilateral regulations on consideration of foreign withholding taxes at fund level are subject to less uncertainty in regard to actual applicability than the regulations governing withholding taxes at asset level. The claim is denied the investor only in France, Italy and Switzerland. In all other countries, it is possible to offset against the final income tax liability. Alternatively, Germany, Ireland and the United Kingdom offer the investor the option of deducting the foreign withholding taxes from the income tax assessment base.

2.2.4.5 Preliminary Conclusions on Taxation at Investor Level

Cross-border heterogeneity in regard to the resulting tax consequences is apparent at investor level as well. The question of when and to which extent private investors are subject to unlimited income tax liability with their investment income in the country in which they reside can often not be answered until it is known whether there is current income or capital gains and whether this investment income is distributed by a fund (partially or completely) or accumulated by it. And it is not unusual to differentiate between various types of funds and subsequently to incorporate consideration of the specific participation relationships between fund and investor. Furthermore, if one keeps in mind that withholding taxation at asset level may also be fund-specific and qualification of the income only rarely takes into consideration the original underlying assets, it can be said that, in most of the cases examined, the fund level is relevant for taxation purposes.

2.2.5 Concluding Remarks on Investment Taxation in the Domestic Case

In the following table we endeavour to categorise the individual taxation systems of the countries examined into five levels of transparency for tax purposes, with each group as homogeneous as possible. To present the results for the domestic investment case in a clear overview, despite their heterogeneity, it is necessary to reduce some of the complexity of the issue to a certain degree and to restrict the information to the essential characteristics of the taxation systems for allocation to the categories.

When assigning countries to the categories, the decisive criterion is whether the income is taxed only at investor level (*groups 1–3*), the income is taxed at both the investor level and the fund level (*group 4*) or only the fund is subject to income taxation (*group 5*). The degree of transparency is determined by the extent to which the taxation system in question attempts to achieve equal taxation of investments via investment funds with direct investments in assets. The transfer for tax purposes of the amount of investment income from the assets is taken into account; it is irrelevant whether the income earned by the fund is re-qualified for tax purposes. The transparency for tax purposes decreases, beginning with the system of taxation only of the investor, which is not affected by decisions relating to appropriation of earnings at fund level (= transparency principle) and progressing to the system of income taxation only at fund level (= separate entity principle).

The systems in which only the investor is taxed are further differentiated by whether all of the income, regardless of appropriation of earnings, is immediately subject to the investor's income tax (*group 1*); whether allocation of the investment income to certain types of income is relevant for investor taxation (*group 2*) and whether charging the investor personal income tax requires actual distribution of income or—in other words—income taxation can be deferred in the case of accumulation (*group 3*).

When evaluating the question of whether taxation occurs at fund level, a potential individual (corporation) tax liability is taken into account. This is also considered to be the case when only part of the income or only certain types of income are subject to taxation at fund level. When a country offers tax privileges for the fund, this is applied as the basis of allocation. This is significant in the cases of the Netherlands (qualification as VBI or FBI), Spain (qualification for preferential corporation tax system) and the USA (qualification as RIC). In regard to taxation at

2.2 Taxation of Income from Investment Funds

Table 2.17 Characterisation of the investment tax systems examined

Group	Description of taxation system	Country
1	*Completely transparent taxation* of investor • Income taxation at investor level • *Appropriation of earnings* is *irrelevant* for taxation, so the system does *not* facilitate *deferment of taxation*	• *Denmark* ("Distributing funds" that do not hold only bonds; investment companies) • *Germany* (interest) • *Luxembourg* (FCP) • *Netherlands* • *Switzerland* (dividends and interest from distribution funds; mixed and cumulative funds) • *USA* (distributed capital gains) • *United Kingdom* (dividends)
2	*Partially transparent taxation* of investor • Income taxation at investor level • *Type of income and appropriation of earnings* is *relevant* for taxation	• *Germany* (capital gains) • *France* • *Italy* • *Switzerland* (capital gains from distribution funds) • *USA* (distributed dividends and interest)
3	*Intransparent taxation* of investor • Income taxation at investor level • *Only the appropriation of earnings* is *relevant* for taxation, so the system facilitates *deferment of taxation*	• *Denmark* ("Distributing funds" investing solely in bonds) • *Ireland* • *Japan* (contract type) • *Luxembourg* (SICAV) • *Poland*
4	*Double taxation* • Income taxation at investor level and • Income taxation at *fund level*	• *Germany* (dividends) • *Japan* (company type) • *Spain* • *USA* (accumulation) • *United Kingdom* (interest)
5	"*Business tax*" (sole taxation at fund level) • Income taxation *only* at fund level • *Appropriation of earnings* is *irrelevant* for taxation	

(Transparency decreases from group 1 to group 5)

investor level, all of the taxes levied on distributed and/or accumulated income on behalf of the investor, including any withholding taxes at fund level, are taken into account along with the assessed income tax.

As Table 2.17 shows, there is no predominant degree of transparency in the countries examined for this study. The systems range from completely transparent tax regimes (group 1) to intransparent systems with taxation at the fund and investor level (group 4). A uniform tax system can be identified for only six countries: these countries do not differentiate between types of funds and income. A system that covers all of the investment strategies of interest here could not be found in the remaining countries; rather differentiating consideration is called for in this respect.

None of the countries examined have a completely intransparent system in which only the fund is taxed (group 5). Taxation consequences tie in at investor level in all of the countries. Taxation here depends partially on the appropriation of earnings at fund level and on the qualification of income at investor level.

Seven tax regimes can be allocated to the *first group* (no income taxation at fund level). In these cases taxation of the investment income cannot be deferred:
- In *Denmark* funds which are particularly qualified for tax purposes (so-called "distributing funds") are to be distinguished from the basic form of the "investment companies". With units in an investment company, the annual gain in fund capital is taxed at investor level. "Distributing funds" are obligated to calculate a fictitious minimum distribution to the investors, which entails deduction of withholding tax on behalf of the investor, regardless of whether actual distribution took place. The obligation to deduct a withholding tax on behalf of the investor at fund level is waived only for "distributing funds" that invest exclusively in bonds. With the exception of this special case, taxation cannot be deferred.
- In *Germany* the investor is subject to taxation with distributed as well as with accumulated ordinary interest income. This always applies, regardless of whether the investor holds his fund units as personal assets (tax liability is fulfilled by the withholding tax at fund level) or business assets (taxation of 100 % of interest income at the personal income tax rate).
- Investors with units in an FCP in *Luxembourg* must assess the investment income from a fund at their personal income tax rate in the year the income is generated.
- In the *Netherlands*, the average market value of the assets in which the fund invests is taxed at investor level.
- The way in which the fund distributes is decisive for investor taxation in *Switzerland*. While a distribution rate of less than 70 % generally leads to completely transparent taxation of the investor, this applies to funds that reach or exceed this level only to the extent that the fund generates dividends and interest.
- *US American* funds are to be allocated to this group in so far as they distribute capital gains to the investor.
- Finally, the taxation system for dividend income in the *United Kingdom* can be allocated to the first group. Dividends are taxed at investor level independently of the appropriation of earnings.

The *second group* (no taxation at fund level; appropriation of earnings and income qualification are relevant) includes five taxation systems that allow deferment of taxation and thus can only be considered partially transparent:
- In contrast to income from current interest and dividend income, in *Germany* profits that the fund made from the disposal of assets are not taxed until they are distributed to the investor.
- *France* allows the investor to choose between flat-rate taxation of the income at fund level and assessment of income. If the investor chooses assessment, the

2.2 Taxation of Income from Investment Funds

scope of the assessment base for income tax purposes is a factor of the type of income. Accumulated fund income does not pose a tax liability for the investor.
- *Italy* does not levy withholding taxes at fund level until the time of distribution. A proportional rate is always applied, with the exception of certain bonds that benefit from withholding tax privileges. When fund units are held as personal assets, the investor's income tax liability is met in this way. If the units are held as business assets, the income drawn from the fund is assessed—assuming actual distribution has occurred.
- Capital gains from a distribution fund in *Switzerland* are not assessed for the investor's income tax purposes until distribution has taken place. Unlike ordinary investment income, this type of income is not subject to withholding tax at fund level.
- The *USA* levies taxes only on accumulated income at the level of an RIC. A tax liability at investor level is established when the fund distributes income from equity securities and bonds to the investors. Consequently, taxation is a factor of appropriation of earnings and income qualification here, too.

The *third group* is comprised of the countries in which there is no taxation at fund level but in which only the appropriation of earnings is relevant for taxation consequences at investor level. Due to the sole significance of circumstances at fund level, the following six taxation systems are considered intransparent:
- Investors in *Denmark* who choose to invest money in distributing funds are not taxed transparently when the fund's investment portfolio contains only bonds. In this case withholding taxation at fund level is waived, and no assessment for income tax purposes must be made for the duration of accumulation in the fund.
- *Ireland* closely links the investor's tax liability in regard to income from the fund to the condition of distribution. The tax liability is ultimately met by the withholding tax levied at fund level.
- *Japan* exempts contract-type funds from an independent tax liability. The investor has a tax liability only for fund distributions, and the liability is fulfilled with the tax deduction at fund level.
- Investors with shares in an SICAV in *Luxembourg* are not subject to personal income tax as long as the income is accumulated in the fund. Withholding taxes at fund level are not existent in Luxembourg law in this respect.
- *Poland* levies taxes on investors only in regard to fund distributions; this liability is fulfilled by a withholding tax at fund level, due at the time of distribution.
- *Switzerland* at least partially applies taxation to the investor depending on appropriation of earnings, as tax liability is dependent on the distribution rate. If less than 70 % of the distributable profits are distributed, the investors are liable for taxes on the distributed portion as well as the accumulated portion. Because of this, tax deferment is possible for no more than 30 % of the distributable profit.

The taxation systems of five countries are allocated to the *fourth group* (income taxation at investor level and fund level):
- Dividend income derived by publicly traded investment funds in *Germany* is taxed at fund level with corporate income tax and solidarity surcharge. The tax liability of the investor depends on whether the fund units are held as private

or business assets. While in the former case tax liability is fulfilled by application of withholding tax at fund level, in the latter case the investor has to subject 60 % of dividend income to the personal income tax rate.
- In *Japan* company-type funds are subject to an independent tax liability. At the time of distribution to the investor, the fund is obligated to deduct withholding tax on behalf of the investor and with a settling effect.
- Investment funds have an independent tax liability in *Spain*, too. The investors also owe taxes on the investment income distributed by the fund. If the fund accumulates, there is no tax liability for the investor.
- To the extent that a *US-American* RIC accumulates investment income, it has an independent tax liability for the accumulated portion. In addition, the income distributed to the investor poses a tax liability at this level.
- In the *United Kingdom*, the independent tax liability of the fund is always restricted to income from bonds. The investor is liable for taxes on the distributions from the fund, whereby income accumulated by the fund is deemed as distributed to the investor.

2.2.6 Taxation of Income from the Disposal of Fund Units

So far, this study has dealt with taxation of investment income earned by a private investor on units in an investment fund. The study distinguished between ordinary investment income (current income from investment in equity securities or bonds) and extraordinary investment income (profits from the disposal of assets). The tax consequences to an investor related to disposal or redemption of his units in a fund have not been considered thus far. Hence this section deals with the potential tax liability to which the investor may be subject in some of the countries resulting from any profits from the disposal or redemption of fund units. Table 2.18 shows 18 different cases.

Tax exemption may be granted (in certain cases) in only four of the countries examined.

Japan exempts from taxation units in bond funds of the contract type, while subjecting the disposal of units in equity funds of the contract type to a 10 % tax rate. Differentiated tax rates apply to shares in company-type funds: profits gained from the disposal of shares in publicly listed funds are taxed at a rate of 10 %, while a tax rate of 20 % is levied on shares in non-listed funds.

The *Netherlands* do not levy income tax on capital gains from intransparent funds of the FBI and VBI type. In principle, the disposal of units in funds of the legal form FGR/CV considered transparent for tax purposes is not taxable; however, tax liability can occur indirectly by the fact that, when units are disposed of, a proportionate disposal of the assets in which the fund has invested is presumed.

Cases have to be differentiated in regard to *Switzerland*, too. While the disposal of fund units held as personal assets is tax-exempt, the disposal of fund units held as business assets is subject to taxation as imputed liquidation dividend. The investor

2.2 Taxation of Income from Investment Funds

Table 2.18 Taxation of profits from the disposal of fund units in the domestic case

Country in which the investor is located			Profit from the disposal of fund units	
			Subject to taxation	Not subject to taxation
Denmark			X	
Germany			X	
France			X	
Ireland			X	
Italy			X	
Japan	Company type		X	
	Contract type	Bond type		X
		Equity fund	X	
Luxembourg			X	
Netherlands	FGR/CV		X	
	FBI, VBI			X
Poland			X	
Switzerland	Business assets		X	
	Personal assets			X
Spain	Publicly listed fund			X
	Non-listed fund		X	
USA (RIC)			X	
United Kingdom			X	

is subject to a personal, combined federal and canton tax on the difference between the proceeds from disposal and the nominal fund unit value.

Spain waives taxation of capital gains from publicly listed funds; otherwise a tax rate of 19 % applies. If disposal of the units results in a loss to the investor, he/she can first offset the capital loss against the profit from the disposal of other fund units. Any remaining capital losses may be carried forward 7 years.

Without exception, the other nine countries subject the disposal of fund shares to taxation (of varying rates).

Denmark taxes the sale of shares related to investment companies on a mark-to-market basis at a rate of up to 52 %. When units in "distributing funds" are disposed of, the tax rate applied to equity funds is 28 % or 42 %, while all other funds may be taxed at a rate of up to 52 %.

Tax law in *Germany* differentiates between fund units held as personal assets and as business assets when it comes to taxation of capital gains. When the investor disposes of privately held fund units, the tax liability is in principle fulfilled by the 26.375 % withholding tax deduction at fund level; however, the investor can also choose assessment at the individual income tax rate. The full amount of the profit from the disposal of fund units held as business assets is to be taxed at the investor's individual income tax rate and subject to trade tax in so far as the profit is related to investments in bonds; in as much as the profit is related to investments in shares, 60 % of the capital gain is taxed at the individual income tax rate and is also subject to trade tax.

France levies a tax of 30.1 % on profits gained from the disposal of fund units when the exemption limit of 25,830 € is exceeded.

In *Ireland* a tax rate of 28 % is applied to disposals. Irish tax law also applies a recurring tax every 8 years to fictitious capital gains in order to also tax appreciation in the fund units that was not realised by actual sales; the mentioned tax rate also applies to these fictitious capital gains.

The disposal of fund units triggers a 20 % withholding tax deduction in *Italy*. When the units are held as personal assets, this tax fulfils the investor's tax liability. When the units are held as business assets, the income is assessed at the progressive income tax rate, taking into consideration the withholding tax. Any losses incurred from the disposal of fund units are considered to be "other income" and can only be offset with positive income of the same type; this does not, however, include capital gains incurred from the disposal of fund units or current income from holding such fund units.[74] Capital losses that cannot be offset may be carried forward 4 years.

Luxembourg applies the investor's individual tax rate when units are held for less than 6 months, the top tax rate being 38.95 %. There is no tax liability for profit from the disposal of fund units when the units are held longer.

Poland levies a proportional income tax of 19 % on capital gains.

In the *USA*, capital gains are taxed at a proportional rate of 15 %, provided that the units are held longer than 12 months. Where the units are held for less than 12 months, the capital gains are re-qualified as dividends to which the progressive income tax rate applies.

A private investor in the *United Kingdom* is subject to a tax rate on profits from the disposal of fund units that is a factor of all taxable income in that tax year when the capital gains exceed the personal tax exemption for capital gains of £10,600. If the personal income tax rate is a maximum of 20 % (this assumes total taxable income to be no more than £35,000), capital gains are taxed at a rate of 18 %. Investors subject to higher personal income tax rates have to pay 28 % tax on the capital gains.[75]

2.2.7 Draft Reform Proposal for Public Fund Investment Taxation in Germany

2.2.7.1 Motivation for Reform

Achieving tax equality between incomes received from fund investment and that from direct investment in financial assets was part of the intention behind the 2008 German Corporate Tax Reform, when the new feature of final taxation of capital income was taken up in domestic investment tax law. The tax regime emerging from this reform, however, has neither fulfilled the original goal of tax burden

---

[74] Capital gains from the disposal of shares, on the other hand, are considered to be positive "other income"; refer to Crazzolara (2011), p. 31.

[75] Refer to HM Revenue and Customs (2013).

2.2 Taxation of Income from Investment Funds

equality nor does it facilitate administration of income taxation, in particular in the area of publicly traded collective investment schemes.[76]

German investment tax regime currently in force was attested as being exceptionally complex also by the *Konferenz der Landesfinanzminister der Bundesrepublik Deutschland* (March 3, 2011). It was unanimously agreed to set up a working group representing the Federal Republic and the *Länder* to prepare a reform proposal that would take into account in particular the aspects of simplicity and guarantee of tax revenue. A second revised draft was published on February 24, 2012. Key points of this draft will be outlined in the following as far as income from domestic sources is concerned, the taxation of which is subject to quantitative analysis in Sect. 2.3.

2.2.7.2 Key Aspects of the Bund-Länder-Arbeitsgruppe Reform Proposal

According to the proposal domestic funds are to be subject to separate unlimited corporate tax liability, but will continue to be exempt from trade tax. Exemptions to the corporate tax liability will apply where the fund receives foreign dividends, bond income and capital gains. As a result, at fund level only domestic dividends would be subject to corporate income tax and solidarity surcharge thereon at a (combined) rate of 15.825 %.

During the holding period the income tax liability shall in principle be restricted to the fund distributions, according to the proposal. In place of the transparency principle currently in force, the investor will in principle be taxed on cash flows actually received. Upon receipt of fund income tax at a rate of 26.375 % will become due. But in order to also satisfy the second of the reform goals guaranteeing domestic tax revenue, minimum taxation of fund income at investor level shall take place on the basis of a "pre-determined tax base" (*Vorabpauschale*) irrespective of whether the income is retained or distributed. This pre-determined tax base which is a minimum basis for tax liability is calculated according to the following scheme (Table 2.19).

According to this scheme, no minimum taxation takes place if an investor's fund unit has not gained in value during the fiscal year. Neither is the minimum taxation due if the value of the fund unit has risen during the fiscal year, but the investor has received distributions equivalent to or above the risk-free market rate of return on investment. In this context, the risk-free market rate is deemed to be 80 % of the basic interest rate pursuant to Sec 203 par. 2 Valuation Tax Law. In this case the investor's tax liability is based on the actual distributions received.

A minimum taxation is due, however, if the risk-free market rate of return on investment exceeds the total amount of distributions during the fiscal year. In this case a pre-determined tax base exists and depends in amount on whether the total distributions plus the increase in value of the fund unit during the fiscal year equals or exceeds the risk-free market rate. If this is the case (IN + DIS $\geq$ RR), the pre-

---

[76] Refer to Bund-Länder-Arbeitsgruppe (2012), p. 6; Grabbe and Behrens (2008), p. 950 seq.

Table 2.19 Calculation of the pre-determined tax base

	$IN > 0$		
	Yes		No
	$DIS < RR$		
Yes		No	
$DIS + IN \geq RR \equiv IN \geq RR - DIS$			$TB = 0$
Yes	No	$TB = 0$	
$TB = RR - DIS$	$TB = IN$		

IN Redemption price at the end of the fiscal year minus the redemption price at the beginning of the same fiscal year (increase in value of the fund unit during the fiscal year)
RR Redemption price at the beginning of the fiscal year × 0.8 basic interest rate pursuant to Sec 203 par. 2 Valuation Tax Law
DIS Total amount of distributions during the fiscal year

determined tax base is determined as the risk-free market rate of return on investment less the total amount of distributions during the fiscal year ($TB = RR - DIS < IN$). Otherwise ($IN + DIS < RR$), this tax base is limited to the actual increase in value of the fund unit during the fiscal year ($TB = IN < RR - DIS$). In these cases, both the pre-determined tax base and the actual distributions received are subjected to tax in the fiscal year considered.

In order to avoid double taxation of domestic dividends with income tax and corporate income tax, the intention is to introduce a flat income tax exemption amounting to 20 % of the total taxable income at the level of the investor in the framework of a "partial exemption of share income" (*Aktienteilfreistellung*) whereby the total taxable income is calculated as received income plus any pre-determined tax base, if applicable, irrespective of the actual composition of the income. Precondition for this, however, is that the fund making the distribution holds at least 51 % of its assets in shares and therefore qualifies as a "share-based fund" (*Aktienfonds*).

Gains from the disposal or redemption of fund units are subject to the 26.375 % final tax, analogously to ordinary income. In the case that during the holding period the investor was required to pay tax on the pre-determined tax base this is treated as subsequent acquisition costs of the unit and can be deducted from the earnings upon disposal.

2.3 Quantitative Comparison of Tax Burdens

2.3.1 Overview

Our qualitative analysis of the taxation of investment income clearly demonstrated that the differences in the individual taxation aspects between the countries examined outweighed the similarities. But so far we have provided no more than a basic assessment of tax aspects relating to the countries in which private investors may choose to invest. To obtain more reliable results on this issue, the country-specific consequences on tax burden will be examined in the following section. Cross-border investment structures are ignored here, because they cannot be represented universally. Even the analysis of a purely domestic case requires certain restrictions and assumptions.

Because of the complexity of fund taxation and of the matter concerned, this study is subject to a series of restrictions. On this note, we limit our analysis to a partial area of fund taxation and have to exclude several items, some of which may be of considerable significance. Not included in the examination: taxation not dependent on income, taxation of fund management, social insurance and other cost items. The costs of the tax declaration and tax planning are not considered as a part of our analysis. The limitation to essential characteristics regarding the investor facilitates general consideration, but it can under no circumstances point out consequences of taxation and obligations in individual cases. The tax burden comparisons are also based on numerous assumptions, meaning that the resulting conclusions are valid only within these limitations. So the calculated effective tax burdens can merely be considered as tendencies.

2.3.2 Research Methods

The local tax burden related to investment activities via funds is quantified in this study using the measure of investment theory of the effective tax burden. The income from investment in a fund attributed per period to the investor is determined with and without tax for each situation. The respective internal interest rate is calculated for the series of payments over the periods. The effective tax burden of an investment reflects the percentage reduction in internal interest on the capital invested by the investor due to taxation and is calculated as $s = \frac{r-r_s}{r}$, with s as the effective tax burden, r as the internal rate of the investment before tax and r_s as the internal interest rate of the investment after tax.

2.3.3 Model Assumptions

The *model* applied to calculate the effective tax burden to the investor for the individual situations must be founded on assumptions that reduce complexity to facilitate reasonable calculation of the taxation variables. On the other hand, the model assumptions may not prove to be too unrealistic. By focussing on the simulation of a simple, typical investment case, it is possible to derive at least a trend in regard to the tax burdens.

The case examines a natural person as the investor subject to standard taxation of the income from a contract-type and/or company-type fund. The investor, fund and

Table 2.20 Differentiation of situations in the course of quantitative analysis

Criterion	Differentiation in regard to	
Attribution of fund units	Personal assets	Business assets (relevant in Germany, Italy, Switzerland)
Type of fund assets	Stocks (equity securities)	Bonds
Appropriation of earnings at fund level	Full accumulation (except in the USA)	Full distribution

assets are all governed by the same tax jurisdiction. The quantitative analysis has to be restricted to the purely domestic case: classification of individual foreign fund types and the taxation thereof are factors of the specific structure of the details of the vehicle. Moreover, this classification and thus the tax-related consequences are often determined by administrative and supervisory bodies. Thus in the course of such a study, no basis can be developed to determine sufficiently reliable effective tax burdens for cross-border cases. Apart from that, the fund corresponds to the UCITS directive or meets comparable regulations in the individual countries (Japan, USA) and is conceived as a retail fund. There is further differentiation between the characteristics shown in Table 2.20.

The situations examined in the course of quantitative analysis assume that the *investor* is a natural person; juridical persons are not considered. Germany, Italy and Switzerland also differentiate between whether the investor holds the fund units as personal or business assets; the other countries do not require differentiation between personal and business assets for tax purposes. The model investor purchases units in an investment fund on January 1, 2011 and disposes of the units on December 31, 2015, after holding them for 5 years. The calculation is stretched over multiple periods, so any taxation differences that occur are clearly evident in the differentiation of profit appropriation policy. In view of the absolute amount of the units held and the income that the investor has in addition to the fund holding, two alternatives are examined. In the first variation, the investor purchases fund units for 1,000,000 € and has taxable income from employment of 100,000 € per period. A respective base income from a business is assumed for the investor holding fund units as business assets. The second variation looks at an investor who is comparatively less wealthy. This investor purchases fund units for 100,000 € and has a taxable base income of 50,000 €. The base income flows directly into the assessment base for income tax, provided that the individual countries add the fund income to the investor's other income. Thus the investor's personal income tax rate does not turn out to be unrealistically low when progressive rates are applied. If the model were to take only the income from investment funds into consideration, the result e.g. for a German investor could be that, instead of the flat-rate tax, an assessment of the fund income could lead to a lower tax burden. A basic income

2.3 Quantitative Comparison of Tax Burdens

tax exemption could mean there would be no taxation at all.[77] This base income is ignored for calculation of the effective tax burden applied to the investor. Only the income that the investor earns from the investment fund and the taxes thereon are considered. The investor is single, not subject to church tax, has no children and has no expenses that could be considered for tax purposes to be income-related expenses, special expenses or other similar statutory deductions. Blanket deductions for income-related expenses, similar to the blanket deduction for savings in Germany, are excluded for calculation purposes. Losses carried forward from previous years are also excluded. A rate of assessment of 392 % is assumed for the trade tax in the case of a German investor holding units as business assets. This is the average rate of assessment of all municipalities in Germany for the year 2011.[78] For regional taxes of varying rates in a country, the minimum rate is assumed for the calculations when there are no average values available. Net worth and transactions taxes are not taken into consideration for the investor's tax burden. In particular, the potential effects of introducing an EU financial transaction tax will not be scrutinized.

The respective *fund* is conceived according to the directive on Undertakings for Collective Investment in Transferable Securities (UCITS directive).[79] For the countries examined that are outside the European legal framework, the comparison considers funds for which the essential criteria are conceived similarly to the UCITS directive. Conception in compliance with the directive means that, if the fund is licensed in its country of origin, its sales body is granted the right to market units in all of the other countries of the European Economic Area (EEA) with no further conditions. It is assumed for the purpose of this study that the respective fund has the right to market units in the non-EEA countries (Japan and the USA). As specified by the UCITS directive, the number of investors for the investment fund examined is not defined, and the units can be purchased by anyone.[80] However, for the purpose of this study, the total number of investors should definitely be at least 100. Special provisions in the individual countries that are tied into a lower number of investors are thus excluded.[81] The units can be traded daily or redeemed to the investment company.[82] In addition, the fund examined meets all of obligations to supply information and complies with all regulations regarding administration, sales, risk spreading or investment policies and financing, which

---

[77] Refer to e.g. in Germany Sec 32a par. 1, no. 1 EStG (German Income Tax Law).

[78] Refer to Statistisches Bundesamt (2012).

[79] Refer to European Communities (1985); this original directive CD 85/611/EEC has been modified and supplemented by additional directives. For a consolidated text of the directives, refer to the European Commission (2005), pp. 1–48.

[80] Such investment funds are generally referred to as retail funds (differentiating them from special funds).

[81] For example, in Denmark the investment fund has no tax liability itself as soon as fewer than eight investors hold units. Refer to Ottosen and Jacobsen (2008), item 3.3.1.3.

[82] Such investment funds are generally also referred to as "open-end" funds.

are in place in the respective countries and exceed the UCITS directive. These specifications allow the standard tax treatment of income to be examined in all situations. The case in which the income is subject to penalty or flat-rate taxation in the investor's country of residency because the respective fund does not comply with certain rules is therefore not taken into consideration for quantitative analysis.[83] The respective fund begins economic activity on January 1, 2011 with assets of 200,000,000 € to be managed. The investment company does not levy an issue surcharge for purchase of the units. It shall also be assumed that the investment fund does not issue any new units in the time frame examined.

Thus as of January 1, 2011, the investor holds units amounting to 0.50 % or 0.05 % of the investment assets, with a value of 1,000,000 € or 100,000 €. Thus special classifications for tax purposes of the income that apply above a certain amount of holding (e.g. 1 %) are not examined.[84] With the common sizes of fund volumes in conjunction with an average volume of holdings, such high levels of participation are hardly possible anyway. The current legislation, meaning the legal status as of December 31, 2010 (March 1, 2013 in the case of Germany and July 1, 2012 in the case of Italy and the UK) is applied to the calculations in all periods. When analysing the results, however, planned tax rate changes or sunset clauses are considered when they are known.

When the times of creation of the fund and purchase of fund units coincide and disposal of fund units occurs precisely at the beginning of the new fiscal year, calculation is further simplified. In so doing the tax consequences of the income adjustment, the gain from shares and interim profits to the investor that would result from the purchase or sale of units in the course of the year need not be taken into consideration.[85] It is assumed that the investment fund examined does not invest in securities to which special tax rates apply in the respective country.

The fund examined invests only in objects in its own country (domestic). The investment fund's *assets* are stocks and bonds. This means that the assets can be only stocks (equity fund) or only bonds (bond fund), or the assets can be stocks and bonds (mixed fund). Only the pure types of funds are examined for this study. In the case of pure equity funds, the investment fund earns income in the form of dividends and share price gains. The latter can be divided into realised and unrealised share price gains. Capital gains resulting from shifts in the investment fund's portfolio lead to realised share price gains. Unrealised share price gains are the result of price increases in the investment fund's portfolio. The dividends and realised share price gains can be distributed to the investor. When accumulation

---

[83] Refer to e.g. in Germany Sec 6 InvStG (German Investment Tax Act) or, for cases in which the foreign investment funds are not subject to InvStG, Sec 7 to 14 AStG (Foreign Transaction Tax Law).

[84] Refer to e.g. in Germany Sect. 2 par. 1 InvStG (German Investment Tax Act) in conjunction with Sect. 17 par. 1 EStG (German Income Tax Law).

[85] For an overview of the rules governing income adjustment, gain from shares and interim profits in Germany, refer to Jacob et al. (2007), pp. 55 et seqq., 146–175 and 178–217.

2.3 Quantitative Comparison of Tax Burdens

occurs or before distribution, they, as well as the unrealised share price gains, increase the daily trading value of the investment fund calculated by the investment company and the depository bank. Thus accumulated income and unrealised share price gains are not received by the investor until the units are redeemed or disposed of. With bond funds, interest as well as realised and unrealised bond price gains are generated. In the course of the study, the case of complete accumulation as well as of distribution in each period that includes all income attributed to the investor will be examined for each fund (exception: USA[86]).

The same annual percentage return and performance are specified for all of the equity funds and bond funds examined. A total annual return before tax of 10.78 % is assumed for the investment assets in the case of pure equity funds. This corresponds to the geometric average of the annual return of the global stock market index, "The World Index", by MSCI Barra over the years 1969–2007, provided that it is used in the performance index version ("with gross dividends").[87] The latter means that re-investment of the distributable dividends is assumed for calculation of the index. The total return is divided into a dividend yield of 3.23 % and a capital gains yield of 7.55 %. The reference point is the geometric average of annual returns calculated for the "price" version of the MSCI "The World Index". In this version, dividends are not taken into consideration for calculation of the index.[88] For lack of available averages, share price gains are considered to be 50 % realised and 50 % unrealised share price gains. For the pure bond fund, a total return before tax of 6.00 % is assumed for the investment assets; it is divided into 3.40 % interest earnings and 2.60 % bond price gains. The reference point in this case is the annual and coupon return of the previous year reported for the FTSE Global Government Bond Index at the end of October 2008 for all terms.[89] The bond price gains are in turn assumed to be 50 % realised and 50 % unrealised bond price gains.

All of the dividends are examined after potential definitive (corporate) taxation at the level of the distributing company, meaning the amount distributable to the investment fund is examined. Withholding taxes linked to distribution, generally considered at fund level or investor level, are included in this examination. Transactions taxes charged at fund level are not considered.

Taxation usually applies to the income after consideration of expenses. It may be that these expenses are considered as a lump sum or only to a certain limit in some

---

[86] The case of complete accumulation cannot be examined, because in the USA the investment funds examined are obligated to distribute at least 90 % of their taxable income.

[87] The data can be found on the MSCI Barra homepage. Refer to MSCI Barra (2007). The geometric average was calculated for the annual returns over a time of t years applying the following formula: $\sqrt[t]{(1+r_1) \cdot (1+r_2) \cdot \ldots \cdot (1+r_t)} - 1$.

[88] The data can be found on the MSCI Barra homepage: Refer to MSCI Barra (2007).

[89] For the current index data, refer to FTSE (2007). As of October 22, 2008, an annual return of 6.00 % and a coupon of 3.40 % were reported for the last 360 days.

countries.[90] To simplify matters, the deduction of income-related expenses is not considered in this study. So the earned income pursuant to the assumptions is directly attributed to the investor. Treatment of the losses incurred by the investment fund is also not considered.

All payments occurring in a situation are considered inflow in the period of their economic origin. Consequently, tax refunds increase and payments of tax arrears decrease the investor's earnings already in the period to which they are related. Interest effects resulting from the exact times of payment in the respective periods are not taken into consideration. In the case of distribution to the investor, it is assumed that distribution occurs at the end of the year. In the last period, distribution to the investor occurs before disposal of the fund units. Exchange rates and their fluctuations are not considered. In countries outside of the European Monetary Union, applicable tax exemption limits and tax brackets are converted at the interbank exchange rates of January 1, 2011 to be able to determine a progressive tax rate.[91] Table 2.21 summarizes the model design.

2.3.4 Discussion of Calculation Results

2.3.4.1 Limitations of Model

In the course of the quantitative analysis, it emerged that there are considerable variations in the tax burdens across the 13 individual countries. However, in the majority of these 13 cases the tax burden is largely similar in amount.[92] To a certain extent, this similarity follows from model specification which was designed in such a way as to reduce the high complexity of the underlying different cases in the analysis. In particular, certain details had to be omitted from the calculation process when determining the tax bases, e.g. income-related expenses and exemption allowances, and only a selection of domestic taxation scenarios could be taken into account. As a consequence, special aspects of the applicable tariffs and the fundamental taxation concept take the foreground. Consideration of the different concepts constitutes the principal objective of this analysis, thus justifying the limitations imposed. This also explains why two types of funds were differentiated in the quantitative analysis in France and Luxembourg, the FCP and the SICAV, and in Japan, looking at the contract type and the company type. There are no differences in regard to the tax parameters for our quantitative analysis relating to the other countries involved, making further differentiation unnecessary.

---

[90] Refer to e.g. in Germany Sect. 3 par. 3 InvStG (German Investment Tax Act).
[91] Refer to the currency converter of the Bundesverband deutscher Banken (federal association of German banks) 2011.
[92] For the conclusions on the individual countries, refer to the analyses in Chap. 2.

2.3 Quantitative Comparison of Tax Burdens

Table 2.21 Overview of the parameters of the quantitative model

Investor	
Term of investment	January 1, 2011 to December 31, 2015
Amount of investment	1,000,000 € (0.50 % of the investment fund)
	100,000 € (0.05 % of the investment fund)
Income	Distributions from investment fund and profit from the disposal of fund units
	(a) Income from employment/business 100,000 €
	(b) Income from employment/business 50,000 €
Other	Single, no children, undenominational, no income-related expenses, special expenses, no losses carried forward etc.
	No net worth and transactions taxes
	Rate of assessment for trade tax: 392 %; other regional taxes: minimum rate of assessment
Investment fund	
Creation date	January 1, 2011
Creation volume	200,000,000 €
Received income before tax per period	(a) Equity fund
	Total return: 10.78 %
	Dividends: 3.23 %
	Share price gains (realised or unrealised): 3.775 % each
	(b) Bond fund
	Total return: 6.00 %
	Interest: 3.40 %
	Bond price gains (realised or unrealised): 1.30 % each
Income-related expenses, losses and transactions taxes	None
Other	No issue surcharge, no issuing of new fund units
	All investors from the same country
	No investment amounts or securities that require special tax treatment
	If distribution, then at the end of the period
	No consideration of exchange rates and interest effects within the periods
	All payments occur immediately during the period of their economic origin
	Legal status of December 31, 2010 (March 1, 2013 in the case of Germany and July 1, 2012 in the case of Italy and the UK) is carried forward

2.3.4.2 Consequences for the Selection of the Fund

The model makes it clear that, from the tax perspective, certain types of funds offer the investor most favourable outcomes.[93] This applies equally to scenarios 1 and 2. The tax burden of 0 % and 0.51 % within the premises of the model in both

---

[93] It should be pointed out that the tax burden is of course only one of many criteria relevant for making investment decisions. Return, risk and cost or fee aspects are excluded here, however.

Table 2.22 Lowest and highest effective tax burden for fund units in personal assets

		Fund units in personal assets			
		Scenario 1 (investment amount 1,000,000 €)		Scenario 2 (investment amount 100,000 €)	
		Distribution	Accumulation	Distribution	Accumulation
Lowest tax burden	Stocks	5.10 % Switzerland	0.51 % Luxembourg (SICAV)	3.13 % Switzerland	0.51 % Luxembourg (SICAV)
	Bonds	5.10 % Switzerland	0.00 % Japan (contract type)	3.13 % Switzerland	0.00 % Japan (contract type)
Highest tax burden	Stocks	40.28 % Denmark	47.68 % Denmark	40.28 % Denmark	37.09 % Denmark
	Bonds	36.60 % United Kingdom	44.22 % United Kingdom	32.54 % United Kingdom	39.05 % United Kingdom

scenarios in Luxembourg (growth equity funds of the company type) and in Japan (growth bond funds of the contract type), respectively, is of particular interest. These results are due in particular to the exemption of earnings from the disposal of fund units in both countries, meaning that the investor can earn the income tax-free. In this context, capital gains accrued in Japan are always tax exempted. In Luxembourg the units must be held for at least 6 months ("speculation period") in order to be exempted from capital gains tax.

2.3.4.3 Consequences for Tax Burden

When the effective tax burdens are compared across the countries examined, a substantial margin of variation becomes apparent with regard to investment in *personal assets*. Where income is distributed, the lowest tax burden is always to be found in Switzerland. The essential reason is the relatively low combined tax rate to which the investor is subject in Switzerland. As far as equity funds are concerned, the highest tax burden is in Denmark, because a Danish investor faces a relatively high tax rate of income tax. Regarding bond funds, our results indicate that the United Kingdom is the least advantageous country for a domestic investment. In the case of growth funds, the effective tax rate for equity funds of the company type in Luxembourg and for bond funds of the contract type in Japan are lowest showing a tax burden of almost as little as 0 %. Table 2.22 shows these results.

There is also a relatively low tax burden amounting to approximately 10 % at maximum in France (distributing equity funds in scenario 2), Japan (equity funds of the contract type and distributing funds of the company type), Luxembourg (accumulating SICAV investing in bonds), and Switzerland (growth funds), while a relatively high tax burden of more than 30 % is shown in Denmark, Japan (growth funds of the company type) and the United Kingdom (except distributing equity funds).

2.3 Quantitative Comparison of Tax Burdens

In France, the relatively low effective tax burden in the case of distributing funds in scenario 2 is due to the fact that the investor can on the one hand opt for taxation of only 60 % of the dividends from the fund. On the other hand the capital gains realised on disposal of the fund units are tax exempt at investor level as they are below the tax exemption limit. Japan levies only 10 % withholding tax on the distributions of equity funds. This tax rate is also applicable in the case of investments in Japanese funds of the company type, as long as these funds fully distribute their income to the investors. The disposal of the fund units is taxed at a proportional rate of 10 %, too. Income of a Luxembourg investor engaged in an accumulating bond-based SICAV is only reduced by the fact that the small amount of annual subscription tax payable by the fund decreases the value of the fund unit and therefore the gain from its disposal.

The relatively high effective tax burden in Denmark and the United Kingdom can be traced back to the high rates levied. In both countries, there is a high level of progression under the assumptions applied. In the case of distributing equity funds, Denmark applies a flat tax rate of 42 % on income exceeding the threshold of 48,300 DKK. As this threshold is exceeded in both scenarios and as no other tax is due on this income, the tax burden of the two scenarios is the same. Accumulated income, however, is taxed as capital income under a combined tax rate of the health tax, the municipality tax and the income tax. Due to the progressive income tax rate, the overall tax burden in scenario 1 is higher than in scenario 2. In the United Kingdom, the tax rate applicable to income deriving from the investment in bond funds (savings income) is not only determined by the amount of the savings income itself but also depends on the level of income from other sources. Our model assumptions lead to a taxation of the first £34,370 of the investor's income from employment at the basic rate of 10 %[94] while the exceeding part is taxable at the higher rate of 20 %.[95] Since at the same time our model's investor does not earn more than £150,000 in total (even if also the savings income is considered), the total amount of the savings income is taxed at the higher rate of 40 % in all scenarios. In order to calculate the effective income tax rate that can be assigned to the income from the fund, the effects of the employment income taxation are eliminated by determining the relative amount of the total income tax attributable to the fund income only (as already described above). The corporate tax liability on non-distributed income earned by a fund of the company type in Japan at the rate of 42 % accounts for the high effective tax burdens connected with investments in Japanese growth bond funds.

In Germany, Switzerland and Italy fund units in *business assets* are subject to a tax treatment that differs from that of fund units in private assets. Table 2.23 shows the calculation results. When looking at units held as business assets, of these three

---

[94] Our model investor receives in all scenarios an employment income above the threshold of £34,370.

[95] Please note that employment income is to be primarily assigned to the 10 % basic rate band.

Table 2.23 Effective tax burden for fund units in business assets

		Fund units in business assets			
		Scenario 1 (investment amount 1,000,00 €)		Scenario 2 (investment amount 100,000 €)	
		Distribution	Accumulation	Distribution	Accumulation
Germany	Stocks	25.94 %	24.10 %	20.62 %	19.44 %
	Bonds	38.28 %	32.30 %	28.50 %	24.15 %
Italy	Stocks	10.34 %	17.94 %	6.56 %	15.05 %
	Bonds	22.88 %	18.76 %	19.55 %	15.33 %
Switzerland	Stocks	18.91 %	22.81 %[a]	11.19 %	15.64 %[a]
	Bonds	18.91 %	22.81 %[a]	11.19 %	15.64 %[a]

[a]Under the assumption that the investor opts to have the retained income recognized for tax purposes. Otherwise, the withholding tax levied at fund level is not creditable/refundable. In the case of the fund units held in business assets, income from the fund becomes taxable at the investor's level only upon distribution

countries Italy generally has the lowest tax burden with the exception of cases involving investments in a distributing bond fund (insofar from the tax perspective Switzerland turns out to be more advantageous as a location). The highest tax burden of these three countries is in Germany. The reason for this is that, in the case of investment in business assets, all three countries take the investment income into consideration for purposes of assessing the investor's income tax. In this context, a progressive tax scale is applied to the income in all three countries, resulting within this model in the lowest effective tax burden arising in Italy and the highest in Germany. Besides, the tax burden in Germany is also driven by the additional income taxation at fund level.

2.3.4.4 Reasons for the Variations in Tax Burden

The following analyses are based on case constellations involving investment in *personal assets*. In situations in which progressive taxation and/or exemption limits apply, the tax burden is lower in scenario 2, which assumes an investment of 100,000 €. *When scenario 1 and scenario 2 are compared*, it is apparent that Denmark,[96] France[97] and Luxembourg[98] show a relatively large variation in effective tax burden. We observe only a minor difference between scenario 1 and scenario 2 in Switzerland, the USA and, for equity funds and distributing bond funds, in the United Kingdom. In seven countries and thus the majority, there is generally no difference in the tax burdens of the two scenarios examined. The reason for this is the proportional taxation of fund income applied in these

---

[96] In the case of distribution.
[97] In the case of distribution.
[98] With the exception of accumulating SICAV.

2.3 Quantitative Comparison of Tax Burdens

countries. In Japan progressive taxation is not applied to the investor based on the assumption that investment is in a publicly offered investment fund. The result in this case, too, is that only proportional withholding taxes and taxes on the disposal of fund units are levied.

In contrast, a different picture emerges when *distributing and growth funds are compared* across the range of countries concerned. Only in the Netherlands are the tax burdens of these two scenarios identical. There are considerable differences, however, concerning the effective tax burden in the case of Denmark,[99] France (FCP),[100] Japan (company type), Luxembourg (SICAV), and the United Kingdom. Furthermore, our results show similar effects as far as bond funds in Japan (contract type) are concerned. The same holds true for scenario 2 in the case of a French SICAV. In the remaining cases the differences are relatively slight. Besides the time effects of taxation, these results reflect the essential determinants of taxation, which are substantially heterogeneous across the countries. So taxation of distributed income as well as of accumulated income and the capital gains from the disposal of fund units ranges from immediate consideration to assessment of fictitious amounts and exemption. In Germany, Spain, Ireland, Italy, Japan (contract type), Luxembourg (SICAV), and Poland, investors with units in growth funds are always subject to a lower tax burden than those with investments in distributing funds. The advantage of accumulation is particularly clear in the case of a Luxembourg SICAV due to the tax exemption of capital gains in this context. Conversely, the effective tax burden resulting from investment in a distributing fund is generally lower in Switzerland, Japan (company type), Luxembourg (FCP), and the United Kingdom. In the other countries, the growth fund and the distributing fund both offer advantages, depending on the specific case, making an unequivocal statement impossible.

Comparison of equity funds and bond funds offers a similar view. There are significant differences in the effective tax burdens arising in Denmark, France (distributing FCP), Japan (contract type) and the United Kingdom. Slight differences are to be found in all the other cases with the exception of Switzerland, where the tax burden for equity funds and bond funds is equal. On the one hand, this result can be traced back to the tax rates that in many countries differ with respect to interest and dividend income. On the other hand, partial differences are common in the tax treatment arising on disposal of fund units and in regard to withholding taxation at the asset and the fund level. For equity funds and bond funds, the degree of the tax burden differences in the countries examined is essentially dependent on the specific case. However, advantages—sometimes significant—emerge from the taxation rules for bond funds in Denmark, Germany (growth fund), and Japan.[101] As far as equity funds are concerned, tax benefits can be found in nine countries as

---

[99] With the exception of equity funds in scenario 2.

[100] With the exception of bond funds in scenario 1.

[101] With the exception of distributing funds of the contract type.

well as in specific cases in two further countries. This can essentially be attributed to the fact that dividend income and capital gains are generally subject to lower tax rates. In Germany there is only a slight difference in the tax burden applying to equity and bond funds, while in Switzerland investments in equity and bond funds are subject to identical taxation. Although identical taxation is to be expected for the individual cases in scenario 1 and scenario 2 in which there are no differences in the taxation concept, there is still a slight advantage in burden connected with equity funds. This slight difference can be attributed to the amount of income and the way it is attributed to its component parts as resulting from the model assumptions, meaning that small time effects play a role.

Finally, it should be pointed out once again that the calculated effective tax burdens and the conclusions thus reached are to be seen as exemplifying but not representing the full picture in its entirety. Factors outside the framework of this model can have a significant effect on the tax burden in individual cases or cancel out the advantages of the fund forms examined. Such consequences may be brought about by losses generated by the investment fund as well as by income-related expenses at the fund and investor level. In addition, progressive tax rates apply in some of the countries examined, with the effect that the amount invested and the investor's other income can have a significant influence on the effective tax burden. Table 2.24 offers a final overview of the effective tax burdens in the various countries and scenarios (refer also to the country Chap. 3 for more information).

2.3.5 Analysis of the Tax Effects Linked to the German Draft Reform Proposal

In order to determine the expected tax effects resulting from the German draft reform proposal set out in Sect. 2.2.7.2, the quantitative model employed here was adjusted according to the intended changes in investment tax law. The following Table 2.25 gives a comparison of the effective tax burdens, as they apply for the model investor under current tax law and under the draft reform proposal.

First of all, it emerges that, in our model, the tax burden of an investment in a *distributing bond fund* would not be affected by the reform. This becomes immediately plausible when looking at the key elements of the reform proposal. Bond funds would generally be excluded from corporate tax at fund level. Moreover, the framework of a "partial exemption of share income" (*Aktienteilfreistellung*) concerns only funds investing predominantly in shares. Furthermore, in the model employed, pre-determined tax bases (*Vorabpauschalen*) do not arise since the supposed amount of distributions (bond funds are assumed to generate distributable income in the amount of 4.7 % times the value of the fund unit at the begin of the fiscal year) exceeds the required risk-free market rate of return on investment

2.3 Quantitative Comparison of Tax Burdens

Table 2.24 Overview of effective tax burdens

| | | | Fund units in personal assets | | | | Fund units in business assets | | | |
| | | | Scenario 1 (investment amount 1,000,000 €) | | Scenario 2 (investment amount 100,000 €) | | Scenario 1 (investment amount 1,000,000 €) | | Scenario 2 (investment amount 100,000 €) | |
			Distribution	Accumulation	Distribution	Accumulation	Distribution	Accumulation	Distribution	Accumulation
CH		Stocks	5.10 %	5.17 %	3.13 %	3.14 %	18.91 %	22.81 %	11.19 %	15.64 %
		Bonds	5.10 %	5.17 %	3.13 %	3.14 %	18.91 %	22.81 %	11.19 %	15.64 %
DK		Stocks	40.28 %	47.68 %	40.28 %	37.09 %	–	–	–	–
		Bonds	33.20 %	43.09 %	24.70 %	30.98 %	–	–	–	–
DE		*Stocks*	*28.59 %*	*25.84 %*	*28.59 %*	*25.84 %*	*25.94 %*	*24.10 %*	*20.62 %*	*19.44 %*
		Bonds	*25.89 %*	*21.79 %*	*25.89 %*	*21.79 %*	*38.28 %*	*32.30 %*	*28.50 %*	*24.15 %*
ES		Stocks	18.07 %	16.70 %	18.07 %	16.70 %	–	–	–	–
		Bonds	18.76 %	17.96 %	18.76 %	17.96 %	–	–	–	–
FR FCP		Stocks	17.91 %	26.07 %	4.48 %	26.07 %	–	–	–	–
		Bonds	23.01 %	27.74 %	17.06 %	27.74 %	–	–	–	–
FR SICAV		Stocks	28.65 %	26.07 %	10.08 %	26.07 %	–	–	–	–
		Bonds	29.58 %	27.74 %	11.86 %	27.74 %	–	–	–	–
IE		Stocks	25.70 %	24.17 %	25.70 %	24.17 %	–	–	–	–
		Bonds	25.79 %	25.74 %	25.79 %	25.74 %	–	–	–	–
IT		Stocks	18.91 %	17.02 %	18.91 %	17.02 %	10.34 %	17.94 %	6.56 %	15.05 %
		Bonds	19.61 %	18.23 %	19.61 %	18.23 %	22.88 %	18.76 %	19.55 %	15.33 %
JP contract type		Stocks	9.40 %	8.37 %	9.40 %	8.37 %	–	–	–	–
		Bonds	15.67 %	0.00 %	15.67 %	0.00 %	–	–	–	–
JP company type		Stocks	9.40 %	33.66 %	9.40 %	33.66 %	–	–	–	–
		Bonds	7.83 %	32.90 %	7.83 %	32.90 %	–	–	–	–

(continued)

Table 2.24 (continued)

		Fund units in personal assets				Fund units in business assets			
		Scenario 1 (investment amount 1,000,000 €)		Scenario 2 (investment amount 100,000 €)		Scenario 1 (investment amount 1,000,000 €)		Scenario 2 (investment amount 100,000 €)	
		Distribution	Accumulation	Distribution	Accumulation	Distribution	Accumulation	Distribution	Accumulation
LU FCP	Stocks	22.27 %	22.66 %	15.44 %	15.77 %	–	–	–	–
	Bonds	26.29 %	26.74 %	18.21 %	18.53 %	–	–	–	–
LU SICAV	Stocks	22.27 %	0.51 %	15.44 %	0.51 %	–	–	–	–
	Bonds	26.29 %	0.88 %	18.21 %	0.88 %	–	–	–	–
NL	Stocks	16.20 %	16.20 %	16.20 %	16.20 %	–	–	–	–
	Bonds	20.60 %	20.60 %	20.60 %	20.60 %	–	–	–	–
PL	Stocks	17.96 %	16.14 %	17.96 %	16.14 %	–	–	–	–
	Bonds	18.62 %	17.30 %	18.62 %	17.30 %	–	–	–	–
USA RIC	Stocks	21.77 %	–	17.35 %	–	–	–	–	–
	Bonds	22.92 %	–	18.34 %	–	–	–	–	–
UK	Stocks	17.90 %	33.50 %	15.59 %	31.14 %	–	–	–	–
	Bonds	36.60 %	44.22 %	32.54 %	39.05 %	–	–	–	–

2.3 Quantitative Comparison of Tax Burdens

Table 2.25 Comparison of effective tax burdens of fund investment in Germany under current tax law and under the draft reform proposal

Case constellation				Effective tax burden		Trend
				Current law	Draft reform proposal	
Scenario 1	Private assets	Stocks	Distribution	28.59 %	23.76 %	▼
			Retention	25.84 %	21.84 %	▼
		Bonds	Distribution	25.89 %	25.89 %	▶
			Retention	21.79 %	19.27 %	▼
	Business assets	Stocks	Distribution	25.94 %	33.86 %	▲
			Retention	24.10 %	32.38 %	▲
		Bonds	Distribution	38.28 %	38.28 %	▶
			Retention	32.30 %	34.82 %	▲
Scenario 2	Private assets	Stocks	Distribution	28.59 %	23.76 %	▼
			Retention	25.84 %	21.84 %	▼
		Bonds	Distribution	25.89 %	25.89 %	▶
			Retention	21.79 %	19.27 %	▼
	Business assets	Stocks	Distribution	20.62 %	26.57 %	▲
			Retention	19.44 %	25.99 %	▲
		Bonds	Distribution	28.50 %	28.50 %	▶
			Retention	24.15 %	26.08 %	▲

(the calculations are based on the rate of 2.44 %[102] fixed for 2012) in all cases under consideration.

Secondly, the tax burden on investment in *growth equity funds* would fall in both scenarios as far as units in private property are considered (scenario 1 and 2: −4.00 % age points). If the model investor holds the fund units as *private assets*, in comparison with the law currently in force, taxation according to the reform proposal would result in a slightly lower tax burden, owing to the fact that taxation of the pre-determined tax bases attributable to the investor after application of the partial exemption of share income at investor level outweighs the current taxation of deemed distributions at investor level. By contrast, in case of units held as *business assets*, the tax burden would rise in both scenarios (scenario 1: +8.28 % age points/scenario 2: +6.55 % age points). As far as units held as business assets are concerned, the considerable increase in tax burden is due to the

---

[102] Cf. Bundesministerium der Finanzen (2012).

non-applicability of the partial income method (*Teileinkünfteverfahren*), according to which the investor, under the law in force, must subject only 60 % of the attributed fund income to income tax while the remaining 40 % do not constitute taxable income.

The proposed reform, however, would have a beneficial impact on investments in distributing equity funds and growth bond funds carried out by investors holding their fund units as *private assets*. Compared to the status quo, the model investor engaged in a *distributing equity fund* would particularly profit from the application of the partial exemption of share income (*Aktienteilfreistellung*) (scenario 1 and 2: −4.83 % age points), according to which the investor would be liable to income tax on only 80 % of the income distributed by the fund. Under the proposed reform, distributed capital gains accruing to the fund would also be covered by the partial exemption regime without, unlike dividends, being liable to corporate income tax at fund level. The investor would therefore face a considerably lower tax burden in light of our model assumptions.[103] The lower effective tax burden on income from investment in a *growth bond fund* (scenario 1 and 2: −2.52 % age points) would be due to the reform-induced switch from taxation of deemed distributions to taxation of predetermined tax bases, resulting in income tax assessment bases the amount of which, under the assumptions made, would be only about half the tax base under current law. As a consequence, the gain from the disposal of the fund units which is subject to tax would correspondingly turn out to be higher than under currently applicable taxation rules. In the aggregate, the investor would still benefit from the taxation regime as represented in the reform proposal.

If the fund units are attributed to *business assets* of the investor, our calculations indicate a potential reform-induced rise in tax burden for investments in *growth bond funds* (scenario 1: +2.52 % age points/scenario 2: +1.93 % age points). Although the current tax payments during the holding period would again be lower than under applicable law, on disposal of the fund units this beneficial effect would be more than compensated for by the progression effect of the income tax rate, which would have a stronger effect than in the private asset case (where the tax burden on the capital gain is determined by the proportional withholding tax rate). Apart from that, investments in *distributing equity funds* would be more strongly burdened than under current law (scenario 1: +7.92 % age points/scenario 2: +5.95 % age points), substantially owing to the non-applicability of the partial income method (*Teileinkünfteverfahren*).

---

[103] According to our model assumptions, the distributions of the fund are comprised mainly (53.89 %) of capital gains realised by the fund on the disposal of assets, which would not be subject to corporate income tax but which, nevertheless, would fall in the scope of the 20 % exemption for income tax purposes.

2.4 Summary

The objective of this study was primarily to undertake a systematic comparison of the central consequences relevant to income taxation of private investments in retail funds in 13 economically significant fund locations in order to offer—taking into consideration existing domestic and international endeavours to reform taxation of investment funds and their investors—alternative constellations of investment taxation systems compared to the current legal situation, and to provide impulses regarding this topic. In addition, the taxation concepts specific to the individual countries were to be made quickly and easily accessible in a uniform grid in the country chapter (Chap. 3).

The *qualitative analysis* included retail funds that are conceived in compliance with the UCITS directive or are comparable to it. If different civil-law fund constellations are also conceivable in a country, this aspect was respectively considered in the examination. The investors considered were natural persons who could invest in equity securities and bonds via the fund. The *domestic investment case* (same tax jurisdiction for investors, funds and assets) was distinguished from three cross-border cases, the reason being that the study was also to look at whether (if any) deviations in tax burden arise in the event of assets or investors being located in foreign countries.

Since *cross-border cases* naturally involve tax claims from at least two countries, the question had first to be answered as to whether funds could be seen as persons entitled to application of existing double taxation agreements, meaning they could claim the protection granted by the agreement. However, the wealth of conflicts in qualification and uncertainties prevented an unequivocal conclusion from being reached.

Examination of the asset level showed a high degree of heterogeneity in withholding taxation at asset level, both on the merits and in terms of amount. In this context it is notable that, compared to the domestic case, there is a relatively strong tendency for the source countries to levy withholding taxes on behalf of the beneficiary owner of the income from the assets. Investment funds themselves are subject to independent income taxation in only a few countries; besides, the taxation can be restricted to certain types of funds or income and conceived to be dependent on the appropriation of income at fund level. Nevertheless, it must be noted that, due to a wealth of other factors, the fund level is not completely disregarded for tax purposes in any of the 13 countries examined. Rather individual tax regulations directly or indirectly influence income taxation of the investor in that withholding taxes dependent on the appropriation of income are often deducted on behalf of the investor particularly at fund level, and the original nature of investment income is often modified, resulting in re-qualification to income that is subject to different taxation. As a result, it can be assumed that the strived-for equal taxation of direct investment in assets and indirect investment in assets via funds is counteracted by the specific regulations regarding fund taxation.

In addition to the qualitative analysis, a *quantitative tax burden comparison* was performed to achieve a transfer of the qualitatively gained knowledge to reliable figures by calculating location-specific tax burdens for a model investor, with the goal of a more differentiated assessment of the investment tax systems considered in regard to their investment effects. As the interpretation of the calculation results shows, the effective tax burden may vary substantially in respect to both alternative investment in a distributing or growth fund, and investment in equity or bond funds. These results confirm the impression gained from the qualitative examination that legislators have many different possibilities to steer the investment behaviour of private investors towards investment funds (of whatever type) or towards direct investment.

2.5 Annexes

Annex I: Withholding Tax Rates According to Double Taxation Agreements

The horizontal lines represent the countries in which the assets are invested; the vertical columns refer to the countries in which the funds are resident.

2.5 Annexes

Maximum Tax Rates Applicable to Dividends for Investors (Natural Persons), According to Relevant Double Taxation Agreements

	DK	DE	FR	IE	IT	JP	LU	NL	PL	CH	ES	UK	USA
DK		15 %	0 %	15 %	15 %	15 %	15 %	15 %	15 %	0 %	15 %	15 %	15 %
DE	15 %		15 %	10/15/20/25 %	15 %	15 %	15 %	15 %	0 %	5/15/30 %	15 %	15 %	15 %
FR	0 %	15 %		15 %	15 %	10 %	15 %	15 %	15 %	15 %	15 %	15 %	15 %
IE	0 %	Domestic rate applies%	Domestic rate applies%		15 %	Domestic rate applies%	Domestic rate applies%	15 %	15 %	0 %	0 %	15 %	5/15 %
IT	15 %	15 %	15 %	15 %		15 %	15 %	15 %	10 %	15 %	15 %	15 %	15 %
JP	10 %	15 %	10 %	10 %	10 %		10 %	10 %	10 %	10 %	10 %	10 %	0/5/10 %
LU	15 %	15 %	15 %	15 %	15 %	15 %		15 %	15 %	15 %	15 %	15 %	15 %
NL	15 %	15 %	15 %	15 %	15 %	15 %	15 %		15 %	15 %0	15 %	15 %	15 %
PL	15 %	0 %	15 %	15 %	10 %	10 %	15 %	15 %		15 %	15 %	0 %	5/15 %
CH	0 %	15 %	15 %	15 %	15 %	15 %	15 %	15 %	15 %		15 %	15 %	15 %
ES	0 %	15 %	15 %	15 %	15 %	15 %	15 %	15 %	15 %	15 %		15 %	15 %
UK	0 %	15 %	0 %	0 %	0 %	0 %	0 %	0 %	0 %	0 %	0 %		0 %
USA	5/15 %	5/15 %	5/15 %	5/15 %	5/10/15 %	0/5/10 %	5/15 %	5/15 %	5/15 %	5/15 %	10/15 %	0/5/15 %	

Maximum Tax Rates Applicable to Dividends for Companies (Inter-Corporate Dividend Relief), According to Relevant Double Taxation Agreements

	DK	DE	FR	IE	IT	JP	LU	NL	PL	CH	ES	UK	USA
DK		0/5 %[a]	0 %	0 %	0 %	10 %	5 %	0 %	0/5 %[b]	0 %	0 %	0 %	0 %
DE	15 %		15 %	10/15/20/25 %	15 %	15 %	15 %	15 %	0 %	5/15/30 %	15 %	15 %	15 %
FR	0 %	0 %		10 %	5 %	0/5 %	5 %	5 %	5 %	0 %	0 %	5 %	5 %
IE	0 %	Domestic rate applies%	Domestic rate applies%		15 %	Domestic rate applies%	Domestic rate applies%	0 %	5 %	0 %	0 %	5 %	5/15 %
IT	0 %	10 %	5 %	15 %		10 %	15 %	5/10 %	10 %	15 %	15 %	5 %	5/10 %
JP	10 %	15 %	10 %	10 %	10 %		10 %	10 %	10 %	10 %	10 %	10 %	0/5/10 %
LU	5 %	10 %	5 %	5 %	15 %	5 %		2.50 %	5 %	0/5 %	5 %	5 %	0/5 %
NL	0 %	10 %	5 %	0 %	5/10 %	5 %	2.50 %		5 %	0 %	5 %	5 %	0/5 %
PL	0/5 %[b]	0 %	5 %	5 %	10 %	10 %	5 %	5 %		5 %	5 %	0 %	5/15 %
CH	0 %	0 %	0 %	5 %	15 %	10 %	0/5 %	0 %	5 %		0 %	5 %	5 %
ES	0 %	0 %	0 %	5 %	15 %	10 %	0/5 %	0 %	5 %	0 %		5 %	5 %
UK	0 %	15 %	0 %	0 %	0 %	10 %	0 %	0 %	0 %	5 %	0 %		0 %
USA	5/15 %	5/15 %	5/15 %	5/15 %	5/10/15 %	0/5/10 %	5/15 %	5/15 %	5/15/15 %	5/15 %	10/15/15 %	0/5/15 %	

[a] 5 % if company owns at least 10 % of the capital
[b] Lower rate applies if recipient company owns at least 25 % of Danish company

Maximum Tax Rates Applicable to Interest for Investors (Natural Persons), According to Relevant Double Taxation Agreements

	DK	DE	FR	IE	IT	JP	LU	NL	PL	CH	ES	UK	USA
DK		0 %	0 %	0 %	0/10 %[a]	10 %	0 %	0 %	0/5 %[a]	0 %	10 %	0 %	0/5 %
DE	0 %		0 %	0 %	10 %	10 %	0 %	0 %	0/5 %	0 %	10 %	0 %	0 %
FR	0 %	0 %		0 %	10 %	0/10 %	0 %	10 %	0 %	0 %	10 %	0 %	0 %
IE	0 %	0 %	0 %		10 %	10 %	0 %	0 %	0/10 %	0 %	0 %	0 %	0 %
IT	0/10 %	0/10 %	0/10 %	10 %		10 %	0/10 %	0/10 %	0/10 %	12.50 %	0/12 %	0/10 %	15 %
JP	10 %	10 %	10 %	10 %	10 %		10 %	10 %	10 %	10 %	10 %	10 %	10 %
LU	0 %	0 %	10 %	0 %	10 %	10 %		2.50 %	0/10 %	0/10 %	10 %	0 %	0 %
NL	0 %	0 %	0/10 %	0 %	10 %	10 %	0 %		0/5 %	5 %	0/10 %	0 %	0 %
PL	0/5 %[a]	0/5 %	0 %	0/10 %	0/10 %	10 %	0/10 %	0/5 %		10 %	10 %	0/5 %	0 %
CH	0 %	0 %	0 %	0 %	12.50 %	10 %	0/10 %	5 %	10 %		0 %	0 %	0 %
ES	0 %	0 %	0 %	0 %	12.50 %	10 %	0/10 %	5 %	10 %	0 %		0 %	0 %
UK	0 %	0 %	0 %	0 %	10 %	0/10 %	0 %	0 %	0/5 %	0 %	12 %		0 %
USA	0 %	0 %	0 %	0 %	15 %	0/10 %	0 %	0 %	0 %	0 %	0/10 %	0 %	

[a] Lower for interest paid by public bodies

Maximum Tax Rates Applicable to Interest for Companies (Inter-Corporate Dividend Relief), According to Relevant Double Taxation Agreements

	DK	DE	FR	IE	IT	JP	LU	NL	PL	CH	ES	UK	USA
DK		0 %	0 %	0 %	0/10 %[a]	10 %	0 %	0 %	0/10 %[a]	0 %	10 %	0 %	0/5 %
DE	0 %		0 %	0 %	10 %	10 %	0 %	0 %	0/5 %	0 %	10 %	0 %	0 %
FR	0 %	0 %		0 %	10 %	0/10 %	0 %	10 %	0 %	0 %	10 %	0 %	0 %
IE	0 %	0 %	0 %		10 %	10 %	0 %	0 %	0/10 %	0 %	0 %	0 %	0 %
IT	0/10 %	0/10 %	0/10 %	10 %		10 %	0/10 %	0/10 %	0/10 %	12.50 %	0/12 %	0/10 %	15 %
JP	10 %	10 %	10 %	10 %	10 %		10 %	10 %	10 %	10 %	10 %	10 %	0 %
LU	0 %	0 %	10 %	0 %	10 %	10 %		2.50 %	0/10 %	0/10 %	10 %	0 %	0 %
NL	0 %	0 %	0/10 %	0 %	10 %	10 %	0 %		0/5 %	5 %	0/10 %	0 %	0 %
PL	0/5 %[a]	0/5 %	0 %	0/10 %	0/10 %	10 %	0/10 %	0/5 %		10 %	10 %	0/5 %	0 %

(continued)

	DK	DE	FR	IE	IT	JP	LU	NL	PL	CH	ES	UK	USA
CH	0 %	0 %	0 %	0 %	12.50 %	10 %	0/ 10 %	5 %	10 %		0 %	0 %	0 %
ES	0 %	0 %	0 %	0 %	12.50 %	10 %	0/ 10 %	5 %	10 %	0 %		0 %	0 %
UK	0 %	0 %	0 %	0 %	10 %	0/ 10 %	0 %	0 %	0/5 %	0 %	12 %		0 %
USA	0 %	0 %	0 %	0 %	15 %	0/ 10 %	0 %	0 %	0 %	0 %	0/ 10 %	0 %	

[a]Lower for interest paid by public bodies

Annex II: Overview of Income Taxation

The following two tables show a symbol-based representation of the basic tax consequences at the three taxation levels in the case of dividend distribution and retained income. It is indicated here, whether the fund is taxed separately, the assets are subject to withholding tax at the level of the fund (and on the account of the investor), and/or the investor is subject to taxation on his/her investment income. For purposes of diagrammatic presentation the following abbreviations or symbols are used.

$C_{(F)WHT}$	Credit at fund or investor level of (foreign) withholding tax withheld at asset level
$C_{F(I)}$	Credit at investor level of withholding tax withheld at fund level
F	Separate taxation of returns at fund level
F(I)	Withholding tax on returns at fund level on the account of investor
I	Separate taxation of the investor
$T_{[country]}$	Tax rate applied by the country [country]
–	No tax consequences at the corresponding level

The possibility of crediting previously withheld income tax, if given, is indicated. For further details please see Chap. 2.

Basic Tax Consequences in Case of Distribution of Generated Income

	Equity fund		Bond fund	
	Regular income	Capital gains	Regular income	Capital gains
CH	F: – C_{WHT}[1] F(I): 35 % I: T_{CH} $C_{F(I)}$[2]	F: – F(I): –[3] I: – (PA)[4]/ T_{CH} $C_{F(I)}$ (BA)[5]	F: – C_{WHT}[1] F(I): 35 % I: T_{CH} $C_{F(I)}$[2]	F: – F(I): –[3] I: – (PA)[4]/ T_{CH} $C_{F(I)}$ (BA)[5]
DE	F: 15.825 % C_{FWHT}[6] F(I): 26.375 % I: – (PA)[7]/ $0.6 \times T_{DE}$ $C_{F(I)}$ (BA)[8]	F: – C_{FWHT}[6] F(I): 26.375 %[9] I: – (PA)[7]/ $0.6 \times T_{DE}$ $C_{F(I)}$ (BA)[8]	F: – C_{FWHT}[6] F(I): 26.375 %[9] I: – (PA)[7]/ $0.6 \times T_{DE}$ $C_{F(I)}$ (BA)[8]	F: – C_{FWHT}[6] F(I): 26.375 %[9] I: – (PA)[7]/ $0.6 \times T_{DE}$ $C_{F(I)}$ (BA)[8]

(continued)

2.5 Annexes

	Equity fund		Bond fund	
	Regular income	Capital gains	Regular income	Capital gains
DK ("distributing fund")	F: $-^{10}$ F(I): 28 % I: T_{DK} $C_{F(I)}$	F: $-^{10}$ F(I): 28 % I: T_{DK} $C_{F(I)}$	F: $-^{10}$ F(I): $-^{11}$ I: T_{DK} $C_{F(I)}$	F: $-^{10}$ F(I): $-^{11}$ I: T_{DK} $C_{F(I)}$
DK (investment company)	F: – F(I): $-^{12}$ I: T_{DK}^{13} $C_{F(I)}^{14}$	F: – F(I): $-^{12}$ I: T_{DK}^{13} $C_{F(I)}^{14}$	F: – F(I): – I: T_{DK}^{13} $C_{F(I)}^{14}$	F: – F(I): – I: T_{DK}^{13} $C_{F(I)}^{14}$
ES	F: 1 % $C_{(F)WHT}^{15}$ F(I): 19 % I: 19 % $C_{F(I)}$	F: 1 % $C_{(F)WHT}^{15}$ F(I): 19 % I: 19 % $C_{F(I)}$	F: 1 % $C_{(F)WHT}^{15}$ F(I): 19 % I: 19 % $C_{F(I)}$	F: 1 % $C_{(F)WHT}^{15}$ F(I): 19 % I: 19 % $C_{F(I)}$
FR (FCP)	F: – F(I): $-^{16}$ I: $0.6 \times T_{FR}^{17}$	F: – F(I): $-^{16}$ I: T_{FR}^{18}	F: – F(I): $-^{16}$ I: T_{FR}^{17}	F: – F(I): $-^{16}$ I: T_{FR}^{18}
FR (SICAV)	F: – F(I): $-^{16}$ I: $0.6 \times T_{FR}^{17}$	F: – F(I): $-^{16}$ I: T_{FR}^{17}	F: – F(I): $-^{16}$ I: $0.6 \times T_{FR}^{19}$	F: – F(I): $-^{16}$ I: T_{FR}^{17}
IE	F: – F(I): 25 %^{20} I: –	F: – F(I): 28 %^{20} I: –	F: – F(I): 25 %^{20} I: –	F: – F(I): 28 %^{20} I: –
IT	F: – F(I): 20 %^{21} I: – (PA)/ 49.72 % × T_{IT} $C_{F(I)}^{22}$ (BA)	F: – F(I): 20 %^{21} I: – (PA)/ 49.72 % × T_{IT} $C_{F(I)}^{22}$ (BA)	F: – F(I): 20 %^{23} I: – (PA)/ 49.72 % × T_{IT} $C_{F(I)}^{22}$ (BA)	F: – F(I): 20 %^{23} I: – (PA)/ 49.72 % × T_{IT} $C_{F(I)}^{22}$ (BA)
JP (contract type)	F: – C_{FWHT}^{24} F(I): 10 %^{25} I: –	F: – C_{FWHT}^{24} F(I): 10 %^{25} I: –	F: – C_{FWHT}^{24} F(I): 20 %^{26} I: –	F: – C_{FWHT}^{24} F(I): 20 %^{26} I: –
JP (company type)	F: – C_{FWHT}^{27} F(I): 10 %^{28} I: –	F: – C_{FWHT}^{27} F(I): 10 %^{28} I: –	F: – C_{FWHT}^{27} F(I): 10 %^{28} I: –	F: – C_{FWHT}^{27} F(I): 10 %^{28} I: –
LU (FCP)	F: $-^{29}$ F(I): – I: T_{LU}	F: $-^{29}$ F(I): – I: T_{LU}^{30}	F: $-^{29}$ F(I): – I: T_{LU}	F: $-^{29}$ F(I): – I: T_{LU}^{30}
LU (SICAV)	F: $-^{29}$ F(I): – I: T_{LU}	F: $-^{29}$ F(I): – I: T_{LU}^{30}	F: $-^{29}$ F(I): – I: T_{LU}	F: $-^{29}$ F(I): – I: T_{LU}^{30}
NL (FGR/CV)	F: – F(I): – I: 30 %^{31} $C_{F(I)}^{32}$	F: – F(I): – I: 30 %^{31} $C_{F(I)}^{32}$	F: – F(I): – I: 30 %^{31} $C_{F(I)}^{32}$	F: – F(I): – I: 30 %^{31} $C_{F(I)}^{32}$
NL (FBI)	F: 0 % $C_{(F)WHT}^{33}$ F(I): 15 % I: 30 %^{31} $C_{F(I)}$	F: 0 % C_{FWHT}^{33} F(I): – I: 30 %^{31} $C_{F(I)}^{32}$	F: 0 % C_{FWHT}^{33} F(I): – I: 30 %^{31} $C_{F(I)}^{32}$	F: 0 % C_{FWHT}^{33} F(I): – I: 30 %^{31} $C_{F(I)}^{32}$
NL (VBI)	F: – F(I): – I: 30 %^{31} $C_{F(I)}^{32}$	F: – F(I): – I: 30 %^{31} $C_{F(I)}^{32}$	F: – F(I): – I: 30 %^{31} $C_{F(I)}^{32}$	F: – F(I): – I: 30 %^{31} $C_{F(I)}^{32}$

(continued)

	Equity fund		Bond fund	
	Regular income	Capital gains	Regular income	Capital gains
PL	F: – F(I): 19 % I: –	F: – F(I): 19 % I: –	F: – F(I): 19 % I: –	F: – F(I): 19 % I: –
UK	F: – F(I): 10 %[34] I: $T_{UK} \, C_{F(I)}$	F: – F(I): N/A I: N/A	F: 20 % C_{FWHT} F(I): 20 %[35] I: $T_{UK} \, C_{F(I)}$	F: – F(I): N/A I: N/A
USA (RIC)	F: –[36] F(I): –[37] I: $T_{USA} \, C_{F(I)}^{38}$	F: –[36] F(I): –[37] I: $T_{USA} \, C_{F(I)}^{38}$	F: –[36] F(I): –[37] I: $T_{USA} \, C_{F(I)}^{38}$	F: –[36] F(I): –[37] I: $T_{USA} \, C_{F(I)}^{38}$

(1) The withholding tax retained in the amount of 35 % is refunded (domestic case). (2) Excess withholding tax credit is refunded (domestic case). No consideration of foreign withholding taxes. (3) Only in case of distribution on the basis of separate coupons. Otherwise 35 % of tax is withheld. (4) Only in case of distribution on the basis of separate coupons. Otherwise taxed at income tax rate T_{CH}. (5) No consideration of foreign withholding taxes. (6) Withholding tax at asset level can be offset against withholding tax at fund level. (7) Withholding tax is normally definitive, unless investor opts for tax assessment; in this case taxed at income tax rate T_{DE}. (8) Plus trade tax. (9) No tax is withheld in case of a non-resident investor. (10) Withholding taxes withheld at asset level reduce calculated minimum distribution. (11) Provided that fund invests solely in bonds. (12) In case of a non-resident investor, tax in the amount of 28 % is withheld. (13) Taxed on a fictitious calculatory assessment base. (14) In case of taxes withheld at foreign fund level, if any. (15) Credit in the amount of 1 %; the exceeding part is refunded (domestic case). (16) Unless investor opts for the prélèvement forfaitaire libératoire in the amount of 30.1 %. (17) If investor has opted for the prélèvement forfaitaire libératoire, there is no further taxation at investor level. (18) However, not taxable if investor holds (in)directly not more than 10 % of the fund units. (19) Distributed interest are normally treated as dividends. If investor has opted for the prélèvement forfaitaire libératoire, there is no further taxation at investor level. (20) No tax is withheld in case of a non-resident investor provided that his or her non-residency is proven. (21) If the investor resides in a "white list" country outside Italy, no withholding tax becomes due. (22) No consideration of foreign withholding taxes. (23) A reduced tax rate of 12.5 % applies in case of income deriving from government bonds and similar securities. If the investor resides in a "white list" country outside Italy, no withholding tax becomes due. (24) Withholding tax at asset level can be offset against withholding tax at fund level. (25) Withholding tax rate is reduced to 7 % in case of non-resident investor. (26) Withholding tax rate is reduced to 15 % in case of non-resident investor. (27) Provided that at least 90 % of income is distributed. (28) Withholding tax rate is reduced to 7 % in case of non-resident investor. (29) No individual income taxation, but tax liability concerning a subscription tax of 0.05 % on the fund's net assets. (30) Not taxable if holding period is longer than 6 months. (31) Tax assessment base equals 4 % of fund assets' average market value. (32) In case of taxes withheld at foreign fund level, if any. (33) The withholding tax at asset level can be offset against the withholding tax at fund level. (34) No tax is withheld in case of a non-resident investor. (35) No tax is withheld in case of a non-resident investor provided that his or her non-residency is proven. (36) An excise tax in the amount of 4 % becomes due if less than 98 % of distributable income is distributed. (37) A 30 % tax is withheld in case of distribution to a non-resident investor. (38) In case of taxes withheld at foreign fund level, if any

2.5 Annexes

Basic Tax Consequences in Case of Accumulation of Generated Income

	Equity fund		Bond fund	
	Regular income	Capital gains	Regular income	Capital gains
CH	F: $- C_{WHT}^{1}$ F(I): 35 % I: $- (BA/PA^2)/T_{CH}$ $C_{F(I)} (PA)^3$	F: $-$ F(I): $-^4$ I: $- (PA)^5/T_{CH}$ $C_{F(I)} (BA)^6$	F: $- C_{WHT}^{1}$ F(I): 35 % I: $-(BA/PA^2)/T_{CH}$ $C_{F(I)} (PA)^3$	F: $-$ F: $-^4$ I: $- (PA)^5/T_{CH}$ $C_{F(I)} (BA)^6$
DE	F: 15.825 % C_{FWHT}^{7} F(I): 26.375 % I: $- (PA)^8/$ $0.6 \times T_{DE} C_{F(I)} (BA)^9$	F: $-$ F(I): $-$ I: $-$	F: $- C_{FWHT}^{7}$ F(I): 26.375 %^{10} I: $- (PA)^8/$ $0.6 \times T_{DE} C_{F(I)} (BA)^9$	F: $-$ F(I): $-$ I: $-$
DK ("distributing fund")	F: $-^{11}$ F(I): 28 % I: $-$	F: $-^{11}$ F(I): 28 % I: $-$	F: $-^{11}$ F(I): $-^{12}$ I: $-$	F: $-^{11}$ F(I): $-^{12}$ I: $-$
DK (investment company)	F: $-$ F(I): $-^{13}$ I: $T_{DK}^{14} C_{F(I)}^{15}$	F: $-$ F(I): $-^{13}$ I: $T_{DK}^{14} C_{F(I)}^{15}$	F: $-$ F(I): $-$ I: $T_{DK}^{14} C_{F(I)}^{15}$	F: $-$ F(I): $-$ I: $T_{DK}^{14} C_{F(I)}^{15}$
ES	F: 1 % $C_{(F)WHT}^{16}$ F(I): $-$ I: $-$	F: 1 % $C_{(F)WHT}^{16}$ F(I): $-$ I: $-$	F: 1 % $C_{(F)WHT}^{16}$ F(I): $-$ I: $-$	F: 1 % $C_{(F)WHT}^{16}$ F(I): $-$ I: $-$
FR (FCP)	F: $-$ F(I): $-$ I: $-$	F: $-$ F(I): $-$ I: T_{FR}^{17}	F: $-$ F(I): $-$ I: $-$	F: $-$ F(I): $-$ I: T_{FR}^{17}
FR (SICAV)	F: $-$ F(I): $-$ I: $-$	F: $-$ F(I): $-$ I: $-$	F: $-$ F(I): $-$ I: $-$	F: $-$ F(I): $-$ I: $-$
IE	F: $-$ F(I): $-$ I: $-$	F: $-$ F(I): $-$ I: $-$	F: $-$ F(I): $-$ I: $-$	F: $-$ F(I): $-$ I: $-$
IT	F: $-$ F(I): $-$ I: $-$	F: $-$ F(I): $-$ I: $-$	F: $-$ F(I): $-$ I: $-$	F: $-$ F(I): $-$ I: $-$
JP (contract type)	F: $-$ F(I): $-$ I: $-$	F: $-$ F(I): $-$ I: $-$	F: $-$ F(I): $-$ I: $-$	F: $-$ F(I): $-$ I: $-$
JP (company type)	F: 42 %^{18} F(I): $-$ I: $-$	F: 42 %^{18} F(I): $-$ I: $-$	F: 42 %^{18} F(I): $-$ I: $-$	F: 42 %^{18} F(I): $-$ I: $-$
LU (FCP)	F: $-^{19}$ F(I): $-$ I: T_{LU}	F: $-^{19}$ F(I): $-$ I: T_{LU}^{20}	F: $-^{19}$ F(I): $-$ I: T_{LU}	F: $-^{19}$ F(I): $-$ I: T_{LU}^{20}
LU (SICAV)	F: $-^{19}$ F(I): $-$ I: $-$	F: $-^{19}$ F(I): $-$ I: $-$	F: $-^{19}$ F(I): $-$ I: $-$	F: $-^{19}$ F(I): $-$ I: $-$
NL (FGR/CV)	F: $-$ F(I): $-$ I: 30 %^{21} $C_{F(I)}^{22}$	F: $-$ F(I): $-$ I: 30 %^{21} $C_{F(I)}^{22}$	F: $-$ F(I): $-$ I: 30 %^{21} $C_{F(I)}^{22}$	F: $-$ F(I): $-$ I: 30 %^{21} $C_{F(I)}^{22}$

(continued)

	Equity fund		Bond fund	
	Regular income	Capital gains	Regular income	Capital gains
NL (FBI)	F: 0 % $C_{(F)WHT}$[23] F(I): – I: 30 %[21] $C_{F(I)}$	F: 0 % C_{FWHT}[23] F(I): – I: 30 %[21] $C_{F(I)}$	F: 0 % C_{FWHT}[23] F(I): – I: 30 %[21] $C_{F(I)}$	F: 0 % C_{FWHT}[23] F(I): – I: 30 %[21] $C_{F(I)}$
NL (VBI)	F: – F(I): – I: 30 %[21] $C_{F(I)}$[22]	F: – F(I): – I: 30 %[21] $C_{F(I)}$[22]	F: – F(I): – I: 30 %[21] $C_{F(I)}$[22]	F: – F(I): – I: 30 %[21] $C_{F(I)}$[22]
PL	F: – F(I): – I: –	F: – F(I): – I: –	F: – F(I): – I: –	F: – F(I): – I: –
UK	F: – F(I): 10 %[24] I: T_{UK} $C_{F(I)}$	F: – F(I): N/A I: N/A	F: 20 % C_{FWHT} F(I): 20 %[25] I: T_{UK} $C_{F(I)}$	F: – F(I): N/A I: N/A
USA (RIC)	F: 35 %[26] C_{FWHT} F(I): – I: –	F: 35 %[26] C_{FWHT} F(I): – I: T_{USA} $C_{F(I)}$[27]	F: 35 %[26] C_{FWHT} F(I): – I: –	F: 35 %[26] C_{FWHT} F(I): – I: T_{USA} $C_{F(I)}$[27]

(1) The withholding tax retained in the amount of 35 % is refunded (domestic case). (2) In case of funds distributing at least 70 % of taxable earnings ("distributing funds"). (3) In case of "mixed funds" or "accumulating funds" (distribution quota below 70 % of taxable earnings). Excess withholding tax credit is refunded (domestic case). No consideration of foreign withholding taxes. (4) Provided the retained capital gains are booked separately from the regular income. Otherwise 35 % of tax is withheld. (5) Provided the retained capital gains are booked separately from the regular income. Otherwise taxed at income tax rate T_{CH}. (6) No consideration of foreign withholding taxes. (7) Withholding tax at asset level can be offset against withholding tax at fund level. (8) Withholding tax is normally definitive, unless investor opts for tax assessment; in this case taxed at income tax rate T_{DE}. (9) Plus trade tax. (10) No tax is withheld in case of a non-resident investor. (11) Withholding taxes withheld at asset level reduce calculated minimum distribution. (12) Provided that fund invests solely in bonds. (13) In case of a non-resident investor, tax in the amount of 28 % is withheld. (14) Taxed on a fictitious calculatory assessment base. (15) In case of taxes withheld at foreign fund level, if any. (16) Credit in the amount of 1 %; the exceeding part is refunded (domestic case). (17) However, not taxable if investor holds (in)directly not more than 10 % of the fund units. (18) If a minimum of 10 % of distributable profit is accumulated; otherwise no individual tax liability. (19) No individual income taxation, but tax liability concerning a subscription tax of 0.05 % on the fund's net assets. (20) Not taxable if holding period is longer than 6 months. (21) Tax assessment base equals 4 % of fund assets' average market value. (22) In case of taxes withheld at foreign fund level, if any. (23) The withholding tax at asset level can be offset against the withholding tax at fund level. (24) No tax is withheld in case of a non-resident investor. (25) No tax is withheld in case of a non-resident investor provided that his or her non-residency is proven. (26) Plus excise tax in the amount of 4 % if a minimum of 2 % of distributable income is retained. (27) In case of taxes withheld at foreign fund level, if any

2.5 Annexes

Annex III: Sample Questionnaire

Country

Short description of the tax system

Basic Information and Sources of law concerning the taxation of funds

Description and basic characteristics
(.... of investment vehicles complying with UCITS)

Investment supervision

Sources of law

Taxation at fund level
(Topics in this section include various levels of a fund investment, i.e. income inflow into a fund vehicle, the treatment of a fund vehicle itself and the treatment of a distribution to its investors at the level of the fund)

Method of income taxation (tax rate)
(For the UCITS vehicles described above we need to understand whether the vehicles them-selves are subject to tax, i.e. in terms of a sepa-rate income taxation such as a corporate income tax equivalent)

Consideration of losses
(Is a vehicle able to carry forward/back any losses from its investments into assets?)

Treaty access of the fund vehicle
(For the UCITS vehicles described above we need to understand whether these vehicles have access to existing treaties)

Crediting of withholding taxes at asset level
(In a scenario where the UCITS vehicles described above invest into domestic assets is there a WHT and if so, is the vehicle able to credit or deduct the WHT suffered)

Distribution obligation for taxation reasons
(Is there an obligation for the UCITS vehicles described above to distribute a portion or all income for tax purposes?)

Withholding tax (tax rate)
(Are the UCITS vehicles described above obliged to withhold taxes when making distributions to its investors?)

Specific characteristics of foreign assets/investors
(Apart from the pure domestic scenario where a domestic investor invests in a domestic fund which in turn invests in a domestic asset we are asking for specifics in the event the domestic fund invests in foreign assets and a foreign investor invests in the domestic fund. The specifics should cover for instance the treatment of foreign withholding taxes at the domestic fund level ("foreign assets") and the treatment of distributions to foreign investors (e.g. in order to see whether there is different treatment between domestic and foreign investors receiving distributions from a domestic fund).

Taxation at investor level
(At this level we are interested in understanding how any income received from a fund vehicle is treated in the hands of an investor)

Distributed interest/dividends (tax rate)
(When a fund is making a distribution this distribution can either be sourced from dividend and/or interest income (as well as from capital gains; see below). If your jurisdiction applies this distinction please indicate the tax treatment at the level of the investor. If no distinction is made please indicate how, and state whether distributions are treated irrespective of underlying income)

Distributed capital gains (tax rate)
(See topic immediately above; consider now a scenario involving capital gains)

Accumulated interest/dividends (tax rate)
(In some jurisdiction when income which is generated at fund level is not distributed to its investors but accumulated in the fund, this accumulation may be subject to tax although the investor does not receive any physical cash. Please indicate how accumulated income is treated in your jurisdiction. In the event that there is a concept of funds that have to distribute their income/part of their income: how is the accumulated portion treated?)

Accumulated capital gains (tax rate)
(See topic immediately above; consider now a scenario involving capital gains)

Consideration of the withholding taxes withheld at the domestic asset level
(In a scenario where the UCITS vehicles described above invest in domestic assets, a WHT at asset level is applicable, and this WHT is neither deducted nor credited at fund level, is the domestic investor able to deduct or credit this WHT?)

Consideration of the withholding taxes withheld at the foreign asset level
(See topic immediately above; consider now a scenario involving foreign assets)

Consideration of the withholding taxes withheld at the domestic fund level
(In a scenario where the UCITS vehicles de-scribed above have to apply WHT on distributions to its investors, what is the treatment of this WHT in the hands of the ultimate investor; crediting vs. deduction?)

Consideration of the withholding taxes withheld at the foreign fund level
(See topic immediately above; consider now a scenario involving a domestic investor investing in a foreign fund)

Special characteristics of the foreign fund
(Apart from considering the WHT in the topics above are there any additional features/specifics to be considered in the event that a domestic investor invests in a foreign fund, such as different tax rates for foreign investments/different classifications of foreign fund vehicles)

Profit from the disposal of fund shares (tax rate)

References

Aigner D (2001) Kapitalfonds im Recht der Doppelbesteuerungsabkommen. Linde Verlag, Wien

Berger H, Steck KU, Lübbehüsen D, Bauer M (2010) Investmentgesetz, Investmentsteuergesetz. C.H. Beck, München

Bund-Länder-Arbeitsgruppe (2012) Bericht der Arbeitsgruppe "Neukonzeption der Investmentbesteuerung" – Entwurf. http://www.der-betrieb.de/content/pdfft,0,469318. Accessed March 11, 2013

Bundesfinanzhof of June 6, 2012 I R 52/11. DB 65.2012:2253

Bundesministerium der Finanzen (2012) Bewertung nicht notierter Anteile an Kapitalgesellschaften und des Betriebsvermögens; Basiszins für das vereinfachte Ertragswertverfahren nach § 203 Absatz 2 BewG (Circular dated January 2, 2012). http://www.bundesfinanzministerium.de/Content/DE/Downloads/BMF_Schreiben/Steuerarten/Erbschaft_Schenkungsteuerrecht/011_a.pdf?__blob=publicationFile&v=3. Accessed February 27, 2013

Bundesverband deutscher Banken (2011) Währungsrechner - Wechselkurse für 160 Währungen. http://www.bankenverband.de/waehrungsrechner/index-xi.asp. Accessed January 1, 2011

Debatin H, Wassermeyer F (2012) Doppelbesteuerung. C.H. Beck, München

Crazzolara A (2011) Italien: Neue Besteuerung der Investmentfonds. IStR-LB 20.2011, Beilage 31–32

Eidgenössische Steuerverwaltung (2009) Kreisschreiben Nr. 24 - Kollektive Kapitalanlagen als Gegenstand der Verrechnungssteuer und der Stempelabgaben. http://www.estv.admin.ch/bundessteuer/dokumentation/00242/00380/index.html. Accessed March 11, 2013

European Commission (2005) Richtlinie des Rates vom 20. Dezember 1985 zur Koordinierung der Rechts- und Verwaltungsvorschriften betreffend bestimmte Organismen für gemeinsame Anlagen in Wertpapieren (OGAW) (85/611/EWG) (Consolidated text of April 13, 2005). http://eur-lex.europa.eu/LexUriServ/LexUriServ.do?uri=CONSLEG:1985L0611:20050413:DE:PDF. Accessed October 29, 2008

European Communities (1985) Council Directive 85/611/EEC of December 20, 1985 on the coordination of laws, regulations and administrative provisions relating to undertakings for collective investment in transferable securities (UCITS). http://www.esma.europa.eu/system/files/Dir_85_611.PDF. Accessed March 8, 2013

European Union (2003) Council Directive 2003/48/EC of June 3, 2003 on taxation of savings income in the form of interest payments. http://eur-lex.europa.eu/LexUriServ/LexUriServ.do?uri=OJ:L:2003:157:0038:0048:en:PDF. Accessed March 6, 2013

Finanzgericht Niedersachsen of March 29, 2007. 6 K 514/03. IStR 16.2007:737

Finanzgericht Rheinland-Pfalz of June 15, 2011. 1 K 2422/08. EFG 2011:1828

FTSE (2007) FTSE Global Bond Index Series Values - Government Bonds. http://www.ftse.com/objects/csv_to_table.jsp?infoCode=ftbo&theseFilters=0~Bond&csvAll=&theseColumns=MCwxLDIsMyw0LDUsNiw3LDgsOQ==&theseTitles=%20,No.%20Bonds,%20Index,%20Days%20Change,%20Months%20Change,%20Year%20Change,%20Return%201%20Month,%20Return%201%20Year,%20Coupon,%20Yield&tableTitle=FTSE%20Global%20Bond%20Index%20Series%20Values%20-%20Government%20Bonds&p_enco ded=1. Accessed October 22, 2008

Geurts M (2011) Das DBA Irland aus investmentsteuerlicher Sicht. IStR 20(2011):573–576

Geurts M, Jacob F (2007) Französische SICAV: Ansässigkeit nur bei Steuerpflicht – und was ist mit dem deutschen REIT? IStR 16(2007):737–740

Grabbe JH, Behrens S (2008) Investmentsteuerrecht: Einführung der Abgeltungsteuer und andere aktuelle Änderungen. DStR 46(2008):950–957

Haase F (2009) Außensteuergesetz Doppelbesteuerungsabkommen. C.F. Müller, Heidelberg

HM Revenue & Customs (2013) Capital Gains Tax rates. http://www.hmrc.gov.uk/rates/cgt.htm. Accessed January 11, 2013

ICG (2009) The granting of treaty benefits with respect to the income of collective investment vehicles. http://www.oecd.org/ctp/41974553.pdf. Accessed March 6, 2013

Jacob W, Geese T, Ebner C (2007) Handbuch für die Besteuerung von Fondsvermögen. Luchterhand, Neuwied

Kronat O (2002) Die Internationale Besteuerung von Wertpapier-Investmentfonds. Peter Lang – Europäischer Verlag der Wissenschaften, Frankfurt a. M

Lang M (2000) Die Besteuerung von Einkünften bei unterschiedlichen Personen aus dem Blickwinkel des DBA-Rechts. SWI 2000:527–535

Meinhardt S (2003) Quellensteuerbelastung ausländischer Zinserträge trotz DBA beim Direkt- und Investmentfondsanleger. DStR 41(2003):1780–1782

MSCI Barra (2007) Index history. http://www.mscibarra.com/products/indices/equity/performance.jsp. Accessed October 22, 2008

Organisation of Co-operation and Development OECD (2009) Report of the Informal Consultative Group on the Taxation of Collective Investment Vehicles and Procedures for Tax Relief for Cross-Border Investors on the granting on the granting of treaty benefits with respect to the income of collective investment vehicles. OECD Review. OECD, London

Organisation of Co-operation and Development OECD (2010) Model Tax Convention on Income and on Capital (Condensed version July 22, 2010). OECD Review. OECD, London

Ottosen AM, Jacobsen U (2008) Investment funds Denmark. In: International Bureau of Fiscal Documentation (ed) International guide to the taxation and regulation of mutual investment funds and their investors. Online-Database. Amsterdam

Schmidt C (2002) Einkünfte aus Auslandinvestmentfonds bei Anwendung von Doppelbesteuerungsabkommen – Zugleich grundsätzliche Überlegungen zur Relevanz des Abkommensrechts bei der Einkünftezurechnung. IStR 11(2002):645–652

Sorgenfrei U (1994) Steuerlicher Transparenzgrundsatz und DBA-Berechtigung deutscher offener Investmentfonds. IStR 3(1994):465–473

Staiger J, Köth V (2012) Abkommensberechtigung einer französischen SICAV sowie des deutschen REIT. BB 67(2012):2915–2919

Statistisches Bundesamt Deutschland (2012) Gewerbesteuerhebesätze 2011 im Bundesdurchschnitt gestiegen. http://www.destatis.de/DE/PresseService/Presse/Pressemitteilungen/2012/09/PD12_320_735.html. Accessed September 14, 2012

Vogel K, Lehner M (2008) DBA Doppelbesteuerungsabkommen, 5th edn. C.H. Beck, München

Wassermeyer W (2001) Ausländische Investmentfonds im Internationalen Steuerrecht. IStR 10(2001):193–203

Zinkeisen K (2007) Abkommensberechtigung von Investmentfonds. IStR 16(2007):583–587

Country Summaries

3.1 Sources of Information

In the interests of achieving a dependable, complete, and comparable data basis, our survey of primary sources and secondary literature necessarily drew on material in the language of the countries concerned. Since our team is not in the position to understand all the languages covered, the survey is based on a standardised questionnaire and was carried out with the support of the PwC network of international accounting firms. The design and content of this questionnaire is reproduced as Annex III to Chap. 2 (analysis section).

As a first step questionnaires were sent to the PwC network companies located in the countries involved. The responses obtained were then consolidated and evaluated. To check that the data was still valid and correct, and updated wherever necessary, a second round of inquiry was made in spring 2012. In general, the information employed reflects the legal situation as of end 2010. Major changes with relevance to our study (e.g., a recent reform of investment taxation in Italy) have been taken into account, however, with the result that our study is based on up to date data in all relevant aspects.

3.2 Tabular Representation

3.2.1 Denmark

3.2.1.1 Qualitative Description
Short Description of the Tax System

Investment company Investment companies are not subject to income taxation at fund level. However, they are subject to a 15 % tax on dividends received on shares in Danish companies. Investment companies are obliged to withhold 28 % of taxes on distributions, which can be offset by the investors.

(continued)

The taxation of earnings takes place at investor level on the basis of the yearly increase or decrease in the net value of the invested capital. Income determined as capital income is therefore subject to taxation. The top tax rate is 52 %. Profits from the disposal of fund units are subject to taxation accordingly.

Distributing fund Investment companies can opt for treatment as a distributing fund if they inform the Danish Tax Authorities that they intend to apply the relevant rules. In principle, distributing funds as such are not taxable. There is an exception for those funds achieving profits from regular business activities (regular earnings) and where more than eight investors are involved. Dividends, interest and capital gains do not qualify as regular earnings.

Concerning pure share funds and balanced funds, where there are earnings and profits from the disposal of assets at fund level, a withholding tax of 28 % applies, which can be offset by the investors. Distributions from pure bond funds are exempt from withholding tax.

In principle, distributions are subject to tax at investor level. A notional minimum distribution is determined. Dividends, interest and capital gains/profits from the redemption of fund units are subject to taxation, which would also have been taxable in the case of the investors acquiring the assets directly. Losses, which would be deductible by an individual, are to be considered in certain situations. The qualification of earnings as capital income, share income or tax free income is in line with the underlying assets, as far as distributing funds are considered. In the case of investment companies, however, the investor receives capital income, irrespective of the fund assets' original nature. Profits from the disposal of fund units are subject to taxation accordingly.

Basic Information and Sources of Law Concerning the Taxation of Funds

Description and basic characteristics	Investment association. Division for tax reasons: • Basic form: Investment company. • Qualified form: Distributing fund. An investment company can additionally opt to be treated as a distributing fund under the following conditions: – Issuing certificates to the investors. – Calculation of a notional minimum payout. – The fund must opt for taxation of earnings by the investor.
Investment supervision	Finanstilsynet (Danish Financial Supervisory Authority, DFSA).
Sources of law	• No separate investment tax law. • Guidelines for the tax treatment of earnings from investment assets are found in: – Tax Assessment Act[a], – Capital Gains Tax Act on Shares[b] etc., – Company Taxation Act[c], – Tax at Source Act[a], – The Capital Gains Act on debt, receivables, financial contracts etc.[d], – Personal Income Tax Act[a].

[a]Latest changes in December 2008 (April 2008 concerning Investment assets)
[b]Latest changes in September 2008 (December 2005 concerning Investment assets)
[c]Latest changes in October 2008 (April 2008 concerning Investment assets)
[d]Latest changes in May 2008 (June 2007 concerning Investment assets)

Taxation at Fund Level

Method of income taxation (tax rate)	*Investment company:* Exempt from tax. *Distributing fund:* In principle, a particular tax subject exists but in practice exempt from tax.
Consideration of losses	Unlimited loss carry-forward in amount and time.
Treaty access of the fund vehicle	*Danish funds:* Foreign states regularly recognize a claim for a refund of foreign withholding tax, on the basis of the double taxation treaty. *Foreign funds:* Individual case decision. If the characteristics of foreign funds comply with those of the Danish ones, in principle, Denmark recognizes their treaty access.
Crediting of withholding taxes at asset level	*Investment company:* Is subject to a 15 % tax on dividends received from shares in Danish companies. No credit or deduction. *Distributing fund:* Upon presentation of tax card nil WHT is imposed.
Distribution obligation for taxation reasons	*Investment company:* No. *Distributing fund:* • No obligation to distribute. • But required to calculate and report a notional minimum distribution.
Withholding tax (tax rate)	Yes, investment companies and distributing funds must in general withheld 28 % on distributions. No WHT on distributions from distributing funds investing solely in bonds.
Specific characteristics of foreign assets/investors	*Foreign assets:* Foreign withholding taxes, at asset level, reduce the minimum distribution from the distributing fund. *Foreign investors:* • Reduction in the Danish withholding tax at fund level is possible as a result of the double taxation treaty. In this case, there is a regular claim for a refund of the exceeding contribution for foreign investors. • For foreign investors from certain countries[a], there are reduced withholding tax rates under the following criteria: – Investor's certificate registered with the Danish supervision of securities (Vaerdipapircentralen), – Danish bank account available, – Investor submits information about the country of residence to the Danish tax authorities.

[a]Among others, Belgium, Germany, Greece, Ireland, Canada, Luxembourg, the Netherlands, Norway, Sweden, Switzerland, USA, and UK

Taxation at Investor Level

Distributed interest/dividends (tax rate)	*Investment company:* • Taxable. • Taxation on the added value of the invested capital, as capital income (maximum 52 % for 2010 and onwards). *Distributing fund:* • Taxable. • Investors are, in principle, taxed as investing directly (share income: for 2010 and onwards 28 % or 42 %, capital income: 52 %). Classification by type of income is in line with the underlying assets.
Distributed capital gains (tax rate)	*Investment company:* • Taxable. • Taxation on the added value of the invested capital, as capital income (maximum 52 %). *Distributing fund:* • Taxable. • Investors are, in principle, taxed as investing directly (share income: 28 % or 42 %, capital income: 52 %)[a]. Classification by type of income conforms to the underlying assets.[b]
Accumulated interest/dividends (tax rate)	*Investment company:* • Not taxable. • Taxation on the added value of the invested capital, as capital income (maximum 52 %). *Distributing fund:* • Not taxable. Non-distributed income is generally added to the purchase price of the certificate and taxed accordingly.
Accumulated capital gains (tax rate)	*Investment company:* • Not taxable. • Taxation on the added value of the invested capital, as capital income (maximum 52 %). *Distributing fund:* • Not taxable. Non-distributed income is generally added to the purchase price of the certificate and taxed accordingly.
Consideration of the withholding taxes withheld at the domestic asset level	*Investment company:* • As a result of the mark-to-market oriented taxation, an indirect deduction in the tax base is possible through a reduction of the fund units' value with withholding taxes. *Distributing fund:* • No consideration.
Consideration of the withholding taxes withheld at the foreign asset level	Under the assumption that the fund is not considered transparent for Danish tax purposes, the investor will not be able to obtain credit or refund for withholding tax as the investor is not the legal nor beneficial owner of the income. However, the investor would have an indirect deduction as a consequence of the value of the units would be reduced if the fund cannot obtain credit or refund for the WHT.

(continued)

Consideration of the withholding taxes withheld at the domestic fund level	Yes, consideration (credit and refund of excess burden).
Consideration of the withholding taxes withheld at the foreign fund level	Credit should be possible but the income calculated for credit relief purposes must be computed according to a net principle which means that any related costs must reduce the dividend income before Danish tax is calculated.
Special characteristics of the foreign fund	No special features.
Profit from the disposal of fund units (tax rate)	*Investment company:* • Taxed on a mark-to market basis at a rate up to 52 %. *Distributing fund:* • Taxable. Tax rates depend on the type of fund and vary between 28 %, 42 % and 52 % (28 or 42 % for share based funds, up to 52 % for others).

[a]Tax rates for individuals for 2010. Basis for taxation for share income: DKK 0-DKK 48.300; over DKK 48.300 (the amount is double for spouses)

[b]Capital gains from certain fixed interest securities are tax exempt. As from 2010 capital gains from shares come into play for the basis of taxation irrespective of the period of ownership

3.2.1.2 Quantitative Comparison of Tax Burden for a Danish Investor

		Fund units in private property			
		Scenario 1 (capital expenditure 1,000,000 €)		Scenario 2 (capital expenditure 100,000 €)	
Country in which the fund is located: Denmark		Distributing fund	Growth fund	Distributing fund	Growth fund
Fund investing domestically	Stocks	40.28 %	47.68 %	40.28 %	37.09 %
	Bonds	33.20 %	43.09 %	24.70 %	30.98 %

Analysis

Clear differences in the tax burden arise from the specific case constellations in scenario 1. Investing in a growth fund gives rise to a considerably higher tax burden than investing in a distributing fund. This is due to differences in treatment of these funds for tax purposes. In the case of growth funds the increase in fair value is subject to tax at the level of the investor. Consequently, capital gains not yet realized are taxed, while in the case of distributing funds capital gains are only liable to tax when the shares are sold. Similarly, the increase in fair value of bonds is taxed in the case of growth funds, whereas proceeds from the sale of bonds are tax exempt at the level of the distributing fund. Moreover, in the case of growth funds investing in shares it has to be taken into account that withholding tax becomes definitive. The disadvantageous tax burden for funds investing in shares compared to funds investing in bonds results from withholding taxes levied at fund level from taxation at progressive tax rates as the former are assumed to generate higher returns. Distributing funds investing in bonds also carry a lower tax burden than funds investing in shares if investing domestically. This is due in particular to the general tax exemption for realized gains from bonds and the correspondingly more favorable progressive tax rate.

As a result of the assumptions made as well as the progressive tax rate, scenario 2 shows in general an overall lower tax burden, with the exception of a distributing fund investing in shares. This is because in both scenarios the distributions from the fund are taxed at the separate rate for share income of 42 %, whereas income from bond-based distributing funds as well as income from growth funds is taxed as capital income at the regular progressive income tax rate leading to a lower tax burden in case of a less wealthy investor. The above mentioned effects gain or lose in intensity accordingly.

3.2.2 Germany

3.2.2.1 Qualitative Description
Short Description of the Tax System

Investment funds and investment companies With regard to taxation, investments in investment funds and investment companies are treated equally. Both investment funds and investment companies are independent taxpayers, but they are factually tax exempt. Therefore neither is subject to independent trade or corporate taxation. As far as withholding taxation at fund level is concerned, a distinction must be made as to whether the units in a fund are held privately or as business assets. Withholding taxes on dividends, interest and capital gains from funds are withheld at fund level at 26.375 %, regardless of whether the fund units are held in private or business property. This withholding tax is normally final for fund units in private property provided that the investor does not opt for tax assessment. In the case of units held in business property, the investor is allowed to credit the withholding taxes against his/her tax liability.

Generally, investment income is subject to taxation at investor level. This applies to all distributed and retained interest and dividends as well as to distributed gains from the disposal of assets. These capital gains constitute income from capital assets, provided that the investor holds less than 1 % of the fund units. If the holding amounts to 1 % or more of the fund units, the gains are qualified as income from trade or business. For fund units in business property it is necessary to distinguish between earnings from equity securities and earnings from interest-bearing securities. Regarding dividends and distributed gains from the disposal of equity securities, 60 % are taxable at the individual income tax rate. As far as interest and distributed gains from the disposal of interest-bearing securities are concerned, 100 % of the income is subject to tax at the individual income tax rate. These earnings form part of the taxpayer's income from trade or business, being additionally liable to trade tax. Accumulated gains from the disposal of assets are tax exempt.

Both fund units in private property and fund units in business property are subject to flat rate taxation if certain reporting requirements are not met. Furthermore, extensive regulations for interim profits, stock profits and income adjustments have to be taken into account for unit disposals undertaken during the reporting year.

Basic Information and Sources of Law Concerning the Taxation of Funds

Description and basic characteristics	• Investment fund (Sondervermögen):
	  – Investors have contractual claims to the fund's separate property (contract type).
	  – The fund invests for the account of the investors who have the right to redeem their units.
	• Investment stock corporation (Investmentaktiengesellschaft):
	  – Investors acquire shareholder rights (company type).
	  – The fund invests for its own account; the shareholders have the right to redeem their shares.

Investment supervision	Bundesanstalt für Finanzdienstleistungsaufsicht (BaFin).

Sources of law	• Investment Tax Act (InvStG).
	• Law furthermore applicable:
	  – Income Tax Act (EStG).
	  – Corporation Tax Act (KStG).
	  – Trade Tax Act (GewStG).
	  – General Tax Act (AO).
	• Investment Act (InvG) regarding civil law and regulatory provisions.

Taxation at Fund Level

Method of income taxation (tax rate)	Individual corporation tax liability: • Dividends are taxable (15.825 %). • Interest and capital gains are tax-exempt.
Consideration of losses	• Unlimited loss carry-forward in amount and time. • Offsetting only against income with the same source.

Treaty access of the fund vehicle	*German investment funds and investment corporations:*
	• Generally not covered by double taxation agreements, owing to the fact that these vehicles are seen as transparent entities.
	• Exception: Double taxation agreement with France and Switzerland.
	Foreign funds:
	• Company-type: Generally covered by taxation agreements under the following circumstances:
	  – No personal tax exemption.
	  – Qualified as an eligible subject in respect to the relevant double taxation agreements.
	  – Residence in the foreign contracting state.
	• Contract type: No information.

Crediting of withholding taxes at asset level	N/A.
Distribution obligation for taxation reasons	No.
Withholding tax (tax rate)	*Private property:* Yes, withholding taxes on capital yields/withholding tax on specific interest income with a final effect for distributed and accumulated[a] dividends, interest and capital gains (flat rate withholding tax 25 % plus 5.5 % solidarity surcharge). Earnings are considered as capital income.[b] *Business property:* Yes, withholding taxes on capital yields/on specific interest income on distributed and accumulated[a] dividends, interest and capital gains (25 % plus 5.5 % solidarity surcharge); no final effect. Earnings are considered as business income.
Specific characteristics of foreign assets/investors	*Foreign assets:* German withholding taxes at fund level can be reduced by the creditable foreign withholding tax. *Foreign investors:* In respect of interest, gains from the disposal of assets, and gains resulting from forward contracts traded by a German bank, no tax is withheld.

[a]The taxation of strike prices for covered calls, forward contracts and capital gains only applies in case of distribution
[b]Trade or business income, if the investor holds at least 1 % of fund units

Taxation at Investor Level

Distributed interest/dividends (tax rate)	*Private property:*
	• Given compliance with announcement and publication requirements according to Sect. 5 InvStG: Liable in principle to income tax. Tax liability is normally settled by final withholding tax. However, the investor has the possibility to opt for tax assessment at the individual progressive tax rate.
	• If announcement and publication requirements according to Sect. 5 InvStG are not met: Subject to income tax. In addition to distributed income, tax liability is extended to cover 70 % of the difference between the first and the last redemption price fixed in the calendar year, at least 6 % of the latter (punitive taxation/lump sum taxation).
	Business property:
	• Given compliance with announcement and publication requirements according to Sect. 5 InvStG:
	  – Liable to income tax. Dividends (60 %) and interest (100 %) are subject to the individual progressive taxation.
	  – Subject to trade taxation.
	• If announcement and publication requirements according to Sect. 5 InvStG are not met: Subject to income taxation. In addition to distributed income, tax liability is extended to cover 70 % of the difference between the first and the last redemption price fixed in the calendar year, at least 6 % of the latter (punitive taxation/lump sum taxation).

Distributed capital gains (tax rate)	*Private property:*
	• Given compliance with announcement and publication requirements according to Sect. 5 InvStG: Subject in principle to income taxation. Tax liability is settled by the flat rate withholding tax. The investor has also the possibility to opt for tax assessment at the individual progressive tax rate.
	• If announcement and publication requirements according to Sect. 5 InvStG are not met: Subject to income taxation. In addition to distributed income, tax liability is extended to cover 70 % of the difference between the first and the last redemption price fixed in the calendar year, at least 6 % of the latter (punitive taxation/lump sum taxation).
	Business property:
	• Given compliance of announcement and publication requirements according to Sect. 5 InvStG:
	  – Liable to income taxation. Capital gains from the disposal of equity securities (60 %) and interest-bearing securities (100 %) are subject to the individual progressive tax rate.
	  – Subject to trade taxation.

(continued)

3.2 Tabular Representation

	• If announcement and publication requirements according to Sect. 5 InvStG are not met: Subject to income taxation. In addition to distributed income, tax liability is extended to cover 70 % of the difference between the first and the last redemption price fixed in the calendar year, at least 6 % of the latter (punitive taxation/lump sum taxation).
Accumulated interest/dividends[a] (tax rate)	*Private property:* • Given compliance of announcement and publication requirements according to Sect. 5 InvStG: Subject in principle to income taxation. Tax liability is normally settled by the flat rate withholding tax. The investor has also the possibility to opt for tax assessment at the individual progressive tax rate. • If announcement and publication requirements according to Sect. 5 InvStG are not met: Subject to income taxation. In addition to distributed income, tax liability is extended to cover 70 % of the difference between the first and the last redemption price fixed in the calendar year, at least 6 % of the latter (punitive taxation/lump sum taxation). *Business property:* • Given compliance with announcement and publication requirements according to Sect. 5 InvStG: – Liable to income taxation. Dividends (60 %) and interest (100 %) are subject to the individual progressive tax rate. – Subject to trade taxation. • If announcement and publication requirements according to Sect. 5 InvStG are not met: Subject to income taxation. In addition to distributed income, tax liability is extended to cover 70 % of the difference between the first and the last redemption price fixed in the calendar year, at least 6 % of the latter (punitive taxation/lump sum taxation).
Accumulated capital gains (tax rate)	Not taxable.
Consideration of the withholding taxes withheld at the domestic asset level	N/A.
Consideration of the withholding taxes withheld at the foreign asset level	No.
Consideration of the withholding taxes withheld at the domestic fund level	*Private property:* Due to withholding tax being final at the domestic fund level, no possibility of taking this into account. *Business property:* Yes, credit/refund.
Consideration of the withholding taxes withheld at the foreign fund level	Yes. Credit or deduction if the withholding taxes are attributable to taxable income in Germany.
Special characteristics of the foreign fund	Two categories of foreign funds are distinguished: *Transparent funds:* • Qualification as transparent through compliance with announcement and publication requirements according to Sect. 5 InvStG.

(continued)

	• Withholding tax on capital yields/special interest is to be retained by the German paying agency. • Foreign withholding tax can either be credited against or deducted from tax payable at investor level, or be considered as business expenses at fund level (option). • Otherwise income is subject to taxation as in domestic cases. *Non-transparent funds:* • Qualified as non-transparent if announcement and publication requirements according to Sect. 5 InvStG are not met. • Withholding tax on capital yields/special interest is to be retained by the German paying agency. • Foreign withholding tax can either be credited against or deducted from tax payable at investor level, or be considered as business expenses at fund level (option). • Otherwise income is subject to taxation as in domestic cases.
Profit from the disposal of fund units (tax rate)	*Private property:* • Subject in principle to income taxation. Tax liability is normally settled by the flat rate withholding tax. The investor has also the possibility to opt for tax assessment at the individual progressive tax rate. • Tax base is the difference between historical costs and the selling/redemption price plus earnings considered to be equivalent to dividends. • Regarding the taxation of interest ("interim profit"[b]), dividends, and capital gains ("stock profits"[c]), as well as a possible income adjustment,[c] extensive regulations have to be taken into account where units are disposed of during the year.[c] *Business property:* • Subject to the individual progressive tax rate. • Subject to trade taxation. • Tax base is the difference between historical costs and the selling/redemption price plus earnings considered to be equivalent to dividends. • Regarding the taxation of interest ("interim profit"[b]), dividends, and capital gains ("stock profits"[c]), as well as a possible income adjustment[c], extensive regulations have to be taken into account where units are disposed of during the year.[c]

[a]Dividend equivalent gains, Sect. 2 InvStG
[b]Sect. 1 par. 4 InvStG
[c]Sect. 8 InvStG

3.2.2.2 Quantitative Comparison of Tax Burden for a German Investor

Country in which the fund is located: Germany		Fund units in private property				Fund units in business property			
		Scenario 1 (capital expenditure 1,000,000 €)		Scenario 2 (capital expenditure 100,000 €)		Scenario 1 (capital expenditure 1,000,000 €)		Scenario 2 (capital expenditure 100,000 €)	
		Distribution	Retention	Distribution	Retention	Distribution	Retention	Distribution	Retention
Fund investing domestically	Stocks	28.59 %	25.84 %	28.59 %	25.84 %	25.94 %	24.10 %	20.62 %	19.44 %
	Bonds	25.89 %	21.79 %	25.89 %	21.79 %	38.28 %	32.30 %	28.50 %	24.15 %

Analysis

The several case constellations of scenario 1 reveal clear differences between the tax burdens of German taxpayers investing in domestic funds. All case constellations show that investing in a growth fund leads to a lower tax burden than investing in a distributing fund. The reason for this advantage lies in the fact that retention of realized capital gains at fund level is tax exempt. Due to the additional taxation of equity funds with corporate income tax, clear benefit for bond funds results in terms of tax burden.

Qualification of the equity fund investment as a business asset brings the investor several advantages. The interaction of the partial income system and the assessment of income for tax purposes taking place in the context of a business asset leads to a lower burden than applying a flat-rate withholding tax, to which investments in equity fund shares held in private property are subject. In the case of bond fund shares held either in private or in business property the contrary effect is produced. Assets held in business property do not benefit from the advantages of the partial income system but are subject to the standard progressive income tax rate ranging between some 14 % and 45 %. Furthermore, liquidity problems often occur in the case of growth fund shares held in business property. Where the tax payable on retained earning exceeds the withholding tax for fictive distributions at fund level, the investor has to pay the difference without receiving a dividend from the fund. Earnings are retained at fund level after withholding taxes have been deducted.

Scenario 2 shows no differences in tax burden for investments held in private property as compared to scenario 1. This is due to the fact that earnings are subject to withholding tax and there is no scope for taking advantage of a more beneficial tax assessment. In general, units in business property are liable to a lower tax burden because earnings are subject to the standard progressive tax rate. The above-mentioned differences in taxation of units in private property and business property result in the tax burden decreasing or increasing accordingly.

3.2.3 France

3.2.3.1 Qualitative Description
Short Description of the Tax System

SICAV A SICAV is a corporate entity. However, no income tax is levied at fund level. In principle, withholding taxes only apply where foreign investors are involved. A SICAV is normally deemed to be a person in the sense of double taxation agreements and in principle, therefore, has treaty access. However, this only leads to the possibility of passing on to the investors the credit/refund potential with respect to tax withheld at asset level.

Income taxation takes place at investor level. In principle, distributed earnings are treated as dividends and, as such, 60 % of this volume is subject to a progressive tax rate. If distribution of income is carried out in the form of specific "coupons", classification of income is governed by the underlying assets. In the latter case, the classification of earnings conforms to the assets concerned and may lead to taxation of the entire gross amount at a linear rate (*prélèvement forfaitaire libératoire*). The same holds true for distributed capital gains. The disposal or redemption of fund shares is subject to taxation at the level of French investors under certain conditions only.

FCP An FCP qualifies as a transparent entity. No income taxation occurs at fund level and, hence, no tax is withheld. An FCP does not constitute a person in the sense of double taxation agreement and as a consequence has in principle no treaty access. Taxes withheld at asset level cannot be credited against taxes paid at investor level and, therefore, reduce investor earnings.

(continued)

Taxation of earnings takes place at investor level. Classification of income is governed by the underlying assets. Distributed interest is in general subject to the progressive income tax. Insofar dividend income is concerned, the investor can choose between taxation of 60 % of the distributed earnings at the progressive income tax and taxation of the gross amount at a linear rate (*prélèvement forfaitaire libératoire*). Distributed capital gains are only taxable if an investor holds directly or indirectly more than 10 % of the fund units. The disposal or redemption of fund units is subject to taxation at the level of French investors under certain conditions only.

Basic Information and Sources of Law Concerning the Taxation of Funds

Description and basic characteristics	• SICAV: Investment Company with variable capital. • FCP: Contractual fund. • The two forms are equally commonly represented.
Investment supervision	Autorité des marchés financiers (AFM).

Sources of law	• No separate investment tax law.
	• Guidelines for the tax treatment of earnings from investment funds are found in the following sources:
	  – The French Monetary and Financial Code MFC.
	  – The AMF General Regulations dated November 24, 2004.
	  – The French Commercial Code.
	  – The AMF General Regulation.
	  – Decrees No. 89-623, 89-624.
	  – Decree of November 21, 2003.
	  – The French Tax Code, FTC.

Taxation at Fund Level

Method of income taxation (tax rate)	No income tax.
Consideration of losses	Not possible.
Treaty access of the fund vehicle	*French SICAV:* • In principle, has treaty access. • Individual case decision dependent on the wording. • In theory, a SICAV only has the possibility to pass the withholding tax credit/refund to investors. *French FCP:* • In principle, no treaty access. • Foreign withholding taxes reduce the investors' earnings. *Foreign funds:* As far as treaty access is available, the crediting of withholding taxes takes place via offsetting or refunding.
Crediting of withholding taxes withheld at asset level	N/A.
Distribution obligation for taxation reasons	No.

(continued)

Withholding tax (tax rate)	No, unless domestic investor opts for making the gross amount of the distribution liable to the aggregate 30.1 % rate of the *prélèvement forfaitaire libératoire*.
Specific characteristics of foreign assets/investors	*Foreign assets:* • FCP: – 0 % withholding tax on distributions from an FCP to a non-resident investor, insofar the distributed earnings derive from foreign sources. *Foreign investors:* • SICAV: – 25 % withholding tax on dividends according to French law; 0–25 % as per the double tax treaty and 18 % for EU, Norway and Iceland citizens. – 25 %[a] withholding tax on interest according to French law; 0–25 % as per double tax treaties. – 0 % withholding tax on distributions from SICAV investing solely in French-sourced debt securities. – 18 % withholding tax on capital gains (if the sum of the resulting profits exceeds €25,730 in 2009), only in case a foreign investor has kept more than 25 % of their share in the SICAV over the previous 5 years. – Tax credits realized through a French fund can be passed on to the investors. • FCP: – 25 % withholding tax on dividends according to French law; 0–25 % as per the double tax treaty and 18 % for EU, Norway and Iceland citizens. – 18 % withholding tax on capital gains (if the sum of the resulting profits exceeds €25,730 in 2009), only in case a foreign investor has kept more than 25 % of the units in the FCP over the previous 5 years. – Tax credits realized through a French fund can be passed on to the investors.

[a]The withholding tax rate can be 60 % for certain securities, if the identity of the investor is not disclosed. If only French bonds are held, the distribution is in the form of interest for which withholding taxes are not withheld

Taxation at Investor Level

Distributed interest/dividends (tax rate)	*SICAV:* • 60 % of earnings taxable (at 5.5 %, 14 %, 30 %, 40 %).[a] In principle, the earnings represent an income group and are deemed dividends at investor level. • A proportional tax rate of 30.1 % on the gross amount of distribution applies (18 % plus additional social charges of 12.1 %) on the application of the investor. Classification by earnings type depends on the underlying assets provided that earnings can be divided up using separate coupons (only certain income categories are subject to this option).

(continued)

Distributed capital gains (tax rate)	*FCP:* • 60 % of dividends/100 % of interest taxable (at 5.5 %, 14 %, 30 %, 40 %)[a]. • A proportional tax rate of 30.1 % on the gross amount of distribution applies (18 % plus additional social charges of 12.1 %) on the application of the investor. Classification by earnings type depends on the underlying assets provided that earnings can be divided up using separate coupons (only certain income categories are subject to this option). *SICAV:* • 60 % of distributed capital gains taxable (at 5.5 %, 14 %, 30 %, 40 %)[a]. In principle, the earnings represent an income group and are deemed dividends at investor level. • A proportional tax rate of 30.1 % on the gross amount of distribution applies (18 % plus additional social charges of 12.1 %) on the application of the investor. *FCP:* • Taxable (at the rates shown above), if an investor holds, directly or indirectly, more than 10 % of the fund units.
Accumulated interest/dividends (tax rate)	No taxation.
Accumulated capital gains (tax rate)	*SICAV:* • No taxation. *FCP:* • Taxable (at the rates shown above), if an investor holds, directly or indirectly, more than 10 % of the fund units.
Consideration of the withholding taxes withheld at the domestic asset level	N/A.
Consideration of the withholding taxes withheld at the foreign asset level	Unilaterally in principle no consideration. However, the investors are entitled to a credit or refund of tax withheld, according to the relevant double tax treaty.
Consideration of the withholding taxes withheld at the domestic fund level	N/A.
Consideration of the withholding taxes withheld at the foreign fund level	In principle, unilaterally no tax credit would be available. Possible, provided a double tax treaty has been negotiated with fund's state of residence. Withholding taxes exceeding the amount stated in the double tax treaty cannot be credited or refunded.
Special characteristics of the foreign funds	• A tax credit is applied to distributed earnings which benefit from (i) a 40 % allowance and (ii) the global annual deduction of 3,050 € (for married persons) or 1,525 € (for unmarried persons). The French imputation tax credit amounts to 50 % of the dividend payment subject to an overall annual cap of 230 € or 115 € (depending on the marital status of the individual holder). • No transparency principle for foreign funds: foreign fund distributions are deemed to be dividends originating from the state of the fund's residence.

(continued)

	Where withholding taxes at asset level are withheld in a third country, in principle these cannot be credited to the French investor. There is, however, a potential for credit according to the double tax agreement between France and the state of fund residence concerned. • According to the position taken by the French Tax Authorities, earnings from a foreign fund are subject to taxation only when they are distributed to the French investor.
Profit from the disposal of fund shares (tax rate)	Disposal/redemption by French investors is taxable (at a rate of 30.1 %) if the sum of the resulting profits in the year concerned exceeds 25,830 €.

[a]Basis for taxation: 0–5,875 €: 0 %; 5,875–11,720 €: 5.5 %; 11,720–26,030 €: 14 %; 26,030–69,783 €: 30 %; 69,783 € and above: 40 %
[b]Basis for taxation: 0–5,875 €: 0 %; 5,875–11,720 €: 5.5 %; 11,720–26,030 €: 14 %; 26,030–69,783 €: 30 %; 69,783 € and above: 40 %

3.2.3.2 Quantitative Comparison of Tax Burden for a French Investor

		Fund units in private property			
		Scenario 1 (capital expenditure 1,000,000 €)		Scenario 2 (capital expenditure 100,000 €)	
Country in which the fund is located: France		Distribution	Retention	Distribution	Retention
Fund investing domestically (FCP)	Stocks	17.91 %	26.07 %	4.48 %	26.07 %
	Bonds	23.01 %	27.74 %	17.06 %	27.74 %
Fund investing domestically (SICAV)	Stocks	28.65 %	26.07 %	10.08 %	26.07 %
	Bonds	29.58 %	27.74 %	11.86 %	27.74 %

Analysis

Where an investor places capital in a French "*Fonds Commun de Placement*" (FCP) resulting profits are taxed in two different ways. Either the profits are subject to tax assessment, or the investor opts for final taxation at fund level at the combined tax rate of 30.1 %. Capital gains from the disposal of fund units are taxed at a flat rate of 30.1 % whereby an annual amount of 25,830 € is exempt. If an investor holds less than 10 % in the FCP, distributed capital gains are not subject to income tax.

Scenario 1 shows that a distributing FCP may be advantageous for the investor. In scenario 2, in case of distribution the investor in an equity fund would be well advised to apply for assessment of income, which is then taxed at the progressive income tax rate. Only 60 % of the dividend income is subject to taxation. As a result, the equity fund gives rise to a significantly lower tax burden than the bond fund.

Where an investor holds shares in a "*Société d'Investissement à Capital Variable*" (SICAV) all distributions are treated as dividend income at investor level regardless of the original source. Again, the investor can choose between tax assessment and final levy of income tax as described above. Distributed capital gains are taxable regardless of the amount of holding.

In the context of the model results, the assessment option generally leads to a higher tax burden in scenario 1, while in scenario 2 the investor should opt for tax assessment. The reason for this is that the investor is not able to benefit from the advantage offered by the tax exemption when income falls below the exemption threshold, with the result that distributed capital gains are not tax exempted, even in part. In case of retention, SICAV returns are taxed in the same way as FCP income.

3.2.4 Ireland

3.2.4.1 Qualitative Description
Short Description of the Tax System

Investment Company, **Unit Trust**, **CCF** Investments in an Investment Company and Unit Trust are treated identically tax-wise. However, investments in a tax-transparent CCF are taxed differently (all income and gains arise to investors irrespective of whether a distribution is actually made). Investment Companies, Unit Trusts and CCFs are not subjected to individual income tax at fund level. 25 % withholding taxes on distributions are withheld at fund level for Irish resident taxable investors and concerning (realized and possibly unrealized) capital gains, 28 % are withheld. Regarding the determination of unrealized capital gains, where Irish resident, non-exempt investors have held units/shares in the fund for a period of eight consecutive years, they are deemed to have disposed of their fund units/shares acquired for tax purposes. Where the value of units/shares held by non-exempt Irish investors is less than 10 % of the value of total units/shares of the fund, the fund will not be obliged to deduct tax on the occurrence of an 8 year deemed disposal provided that they elect to report certain information to the Irish Revenue Authorities and unit/shareholders. In such circumstances, the unit/shareholder will have to account for the appropriate tax arising on the 8 year deemed disposal on a self-assessment basis.

Earnings are not taxable at investor level. The tax liability is definitely settled via the withholding taxation at fund level in case of distribution. Additionally, the disposal or redemption of fund units is taxed at 28 % at investor level.

Basic Information and Sources of Law Concerning the Taxation of Funds

Description and basic characteristics	• Variable Capital Investment Company; Legal form: public limited company.
	• Unit Trust: Generally launched for Irish, British, US-American and Japanese investors; less common for continental European investors.
	• Common Contractual Fund (CCF): unincorporated body; commonly used for bond funds.
	• Qualifying Investor Fund (QIF) and Professional Investor Fund (PIF):
	  – Subcategories of Investment Companies, Unit Trusts and CCFs for large investors and institutional investors.
	  – Fewer limitations to the financing and investment opportunities.
	  – Higher minimum amount of drawn capital for the individual investors.
	• Most common forms: Investment Company and Unit Trust.

Investment supervision	Irish Financial Regulator.
Sources of law	• No separate investment tax law. • Guidelines for the tax treatment of earnings from investment funds are found in the following sources: – Taxes Consolidation Act 1997 (as amended by subsequent Finance Acts).

3.2 Tabular Representation

Taxation at Fund Level

Method of income taxation (tax rate)	*Investment Company, Unit Trust:* Non-transparent units. No income taxation. (Taxation may arise on income distributions or gains on fund disposals/redemptions in respect of Irish resident investors—see withholding tax section below). *CCF:* No income taxation (transparent units).
Consideration of losses	No consideration.

Treaty access for fund vehicles	*Irish funds:*
	• Individual case decision, dependent on the treaty wording and interpretation of the foreign Fiscal Authority.
	• Often a residency certificate with the following information is necessary:
	  – Fund is registered in Ireland (incorporated).
	  – Management and Supervisory body are in Ireland.
	Foreign funds investing in Irish securities:
	  – Where foreign funds comparable to an Irish corporate or unit trust vehicle which are resident in a jurisdiction that has a treaty with Ireland, they should be able to access treaty.

Crediting of withholding taxes levied at asset level	N/A.
Distribution obligation for taxation reasons	*Investment Company, Unit Trust:* No. *CCF:* In general no, but the income of a CCF is considered income of the investor (irrespective of whether the income is actually distributed).

Withholding tax (tax rate)	*Investment Company, Unit Trust:*
	• Yes, not tax exempt for investors resident in Ireland
	  – Distributions 25 %.
	  – (Realized) capital gains 28 %.
	CCF:
	N/A.

Specific characteristics of foreign assets/investors	*Foreign assets:* Withholding tax at the foreign asset level can be passed on to the Irish investors only in the case of a CCF. *Foreign investors in an Irish fund (which is not a CCF):* If foreign investors submit to the fund a declaration that they are not resident in Ireland, there is no withholding tax. Otherwise, withholding tax at fund level of 25 % or 28 % is withheld, for which the investor can claim a refund within 12 months of the payment having been made.

Taxation at Investor Level

Distributed interest/dividends (tax rate)	*Investment Company, Unit Trust:* N/A. *CCF:* N/A.
Distributed capital gains (tax rate)	*Investment Company, Unit Trust:* N/A. *CCF:* N/A.
Accumulated interest/dividends (tax rate)	*Investment Company, Unit Trust:* N/A. *CCF:* N/A.
Accumulated capital gains (tax rate)	*Investment Company, Unit Trust:* N/A. *CCF:* N/A.
Consideration of the withholding taxes at domestic asset level	N/A.
Consideration of the withholding taxes at foreign asset level	The Irish investor would not be entitled to any form of relief for the tax suffered at asset level, unless the (foreign) fund is deemed to be transparent for Irish tax purposes.
Consideration of the withholding taxes at domestic fund level	• Yes. • Withholding taxes on unrealized capital gains from fund units can only be credited on the tax liability from the final disposal of fund units.
Consideration of the withholding taxes at foreign fund level	Double tax relief may be available in Ireland in respect of the tax suffered, either under the double tax agreement in place between Ireland and the jurisdiction in which the tax was withheld or under unilateral relief provisions under the domestic Irish legislation. Relief may be provided by way of credit or deduction, depending on the basis of eligibility for relief.

Special characteristics of the foreign funds	Differentiation of the foreign funds into three categories:
	• Regulated funds:
	  – Residency in EU/OECD countries, with whom Ireland concluded a double tax agreement.
	  – Identical tax treatment as with an Irish fund (provided that in the tax return the correct information is given): 26 % on dividends/interest; 28 % on capital gains.
	  –"Personal Portfolio Investment Undertaking": 48 % on dividends/interest; 66 % on capital gains.
	• Unregulated funds:
	  – Residency in EU/OECD countries, with whom Ireland concluded a double tax agreement and the fund, is a "Personal Portfolio Investment Undertaking".
	  – Taxation of dividends/interest with the individual marginal rate of tax plus duties; 25 % on capital gains.

(continued)

	• Other funds resident in non-EU/non-treaty jurisdictions: – Income and gains generally taxable at investor's marginal tax rate. – For classification as distributing fund: taxation on earnings as for capital gains (40 %).
Profit from the disposal of fund units (tax rate)	*Investment Company, Unit Trust:* Disposal/redemption taxable (28 %). *CCF:* N/A. *Unrealized capital gains from fund units (exit tax):* • Fund units from non-tax exempt, Irish investors (acquisition after January 1, 2001) are deemed sold every 8 years. • Unrealized capital gains from fund units are taxable (28 %). • With the existence of an Umbrella Fund, the 10 % rule is applicable to the sub funds. • If Irish resident, non-tax exempt investors are in possession of less than 10 % of the fund units and the fund has opted for this under certain reporting requirements, no withholding taxes on unrealized capital gains from fund units are withheld, the investor is obliged to calculate and account for their own tax liability (self assessment tax regime).

3.2.4.2 Quantitative Comparison of Tax Burden for an Irish Investor

		Fund units in private property			
		Scenario 1 (capital expenditure 1,000,000 €)		Scenario 2 (capital expenditure 100,000 €)	
Country in which the fund is located: Ireland		Distribution	Retention	Distribution	Retention
Fund investing domestically	Stocks	25.70 %	24.17 %	25.70 %	24.17 %
	Bonds	25.79 %	25.74 %	25.79 %	25.74 %

Analysis

Where an Irish taxpayer invests in a fund, the tax burden differs between the several case constellations. However, there are no differences between scenario 1 and scenario 2.[a]

According to the model, the investment in a growth fund leads to an advantage. In case of retention this is especially due to the time effect, because earnings are subject to taxation only when the fund units are sold. Furthermore, distributed gains from asset disposals as well as capital gains from the disposal of fund units are taxed at fund level at a flat tax rate 3%age points higher than the tax rate for distributed interest or dividends.

There are no differences between taxation of equity and bond funds. The different burden figures therefore arise as a result of the model assumptions.

[a]The outcome results from the flat rate taxation (flat tax) applicable

3.2.5 Italy

3.2.5.1 Qualitative Description
Short Description of the Tax System

SICAV and Common Fund With regard to taxation, investments in a SICAV and a Common Fund are treated identically tax-wise. Both fund types represent non-transparent entities, which are explicitly excluded from liability to individual (corporate) income tax.

As far as withholding taxation at fund level is concerned, a distinction must be made as to whether the units in a fund are held privately or as business assets. Withholding taxes on the funds' proceeds paid to the investors are withheld at fund level at 20 %, regardless of whether the fund units are held in private or business property. In the case of profits deriving from Italian government bonds and other eligible securities, a reduced tax rate of 12.5 % applies. The withholding tax is final for fund units in private property. In the case of units held in business property, the investor is allowed to credit the withholding taxes against his tax liability.

At investor level, one must differentiate between fund units held in private assets and in business assets. The earnings from units held as private assets are not subject to taxation aside from the withholding tax at fund level. For units held as business assets, 49.72 % of interest, dividends and profits from the disposal of assets are subject to a progressive income tax rate. The previously withheld tax is creditable against the investor's income tax.

The disposal or redemption of fund units triggers 20 % withholding tax at fund level that is again final in the case of units held as private assets and creditable against the income tax in the case of units held as business assets.

Basic Information and Sources of Law Concerning the Taxation of Funds

Description and basic characteristics	• SICAV: Investment Company with variable capital (société d'investissement à capital variable). • Common Fund; most common form.
Investment supervision	• Italian Finance Ministry. • Commissione Nazionale per le Società e la Borsa CONSOB. • Banca d'Italia (Italian Central Bank).
Sources of law	• No separate investment tax law. • Guidelines for the tax treatment of earnings from investment funds are found in the following sources: – The Law No. 86[a]. – The Decree No. 58[b]. – CONSOB Regulation No. 11971[c]. – Treasury Decree No. 228[d]. – The Law No. 410[e]. – CONSOB Communication[f]. – The Finance Ministry Decree No. 47[g]. – The Decree No. 225[h]. – The Law No. 10[i].

[a]Last changed on January 25, 1994
[b]Last changed on February 28, 1998
[c]Last changed on May 14, 1999
[d]Last changed on May 24, 1999
[e]Last changed on November 23, 2001
[f]Last changed on June 28, 2002
[g]Last changed on January 31, 2003
[h]Last changed on December 29, 2010
[i]Last changed on February 26, 2011

3.2 Tabular Representation

Taxation at Fund Level

Method of income taxation (tax rate)	• Non-transparent units. • No individual income taxation.
Consideration of losses	No consideration.
Treaty access of the fund vehicle	*Italian SICAV:* Yes. *Italian Common Fund:* No entitlement to implementation of reduced at source tax rates, because Italian funds, as a result of the missing income tax duty, do not apply as resident in terms of the double tax agreement. *Foreign funds:* • Treaty access with residency in the country of the contract partner. • Treaty access for a lack of residency in the contract partner's country for earnings from Italian assets, which are not allotted to investors resident in Italy, exists generally under the following requirements: – Fund qualifies under the UCITS-guideline. – Fund was founded in an EU state, which recognizes the treaty access of Italian funds accordingly.
Crediting of withholding taxes levied at asset level	No.
Distribution obligation for taxation reasons	No.
Withholding tax (tax rate)	• In general 20 % on distributed earnings. • A reduced 12.5 % rate applies to earnings from government bonds and similar securities. • No withholding tax on accumulated earnings.
Specific characteristics of foreign assets/investors	*Foreign assets:* Italian fund earnings from foreign assets are deemed as Italian earnings for the investors. *Foreign investors:* • Foreign investors from qualifying states ("white list") are not subject to an individual Italian tax liability. • Foreign investors from white-listed countries are exempt from withholding tax at fund level.

Taxation at Investor Level

Distributed interest/dividends (tax rate)	PA: Not taxable. Withholding taxation at fund level is final. BA: Taxable. 49.72 % of the earnings are factored into the taxable income amount of the investor and within

(continued)

	the framework of income tax (IRPEF), subject to a progressive tax rate (23 %, 27 %, 38 %, 41 %, and 43 %)[a]. These rates are increased by a regional surcharge varying between 0.9 % and 1.4 % and a local surcharge varying between 0 % and 0.8 %.
Distributed capital gains (tax rate)	PA: Not taxable. Withholding taxation at fund level is final. BA: Taxable. 49.72 % of the earnings are factored into the taxable income amount for the investor and within the framework of income tax (IRPEF) subject to a progressive tax rate (23 %, 27 %, 38 %, 41 %, and 43 %)[a]. These rates are increased by a regional surcharge varying between 0.9 % and 1.4 % and a local surcharge varying between 0 % and 0.8 %.
Accumulated interest/dividends (tax rate)	PA: Not taxable. BA: Not taxable.
Accumulated capital gains (tax rate)	PA: Not taxable. BA: Not taxable.
Consideration of the withholding taxes levied at the domestic asset level	No.
Consideration of the withholding taxes levied at the foreign asset level	No.
Consideration of the withholding taxes levied at the domestic fund level	PA: No. BA: Yes, credit and refund.
Consideration of the withholding taxes levied at the foreign fund level	No.
Special characteristics for foreign funds	• Italy also levies a 20 % withholding tax on investments in foreign funds (compensating effect only in the case of units held as private assets). • Tax assessment obligation if the foreign fund resides in a non white-listed country.
Profit from the disposal of fund units (tax rate)	PA: Taxable. 20 % final withholding tax at fund level. BA: Taxable. 49.72 % of the capital gain are factored into the taxable income amount for the investor and within the framework of income tax (IRPEF) subject to a progressive tax rate (23 %, 27 %, 38 %, 41 %, and 43 %)[a]. These rates are increased by a regional surcharge varying between 0.9 % and 1.4 % and a local surcharge varying between 0 % and 0.8 %.

[a]Tax rates 2012. Basis for taxation (yearly taxable net earnings): 0–15,000 €, 15,001–28,000 €, 28,001–55,000 €, 55,001–75,000 €, over 75,000 €

3.2.5.2 Quantitative Comparison of Tax Burden for an Italian Investor

		Fund units in private property				Fund units in business property			
		Scenario 1 (capital expenditure 1,000,000 €)		Scenario 2 (capital expenditure 100,000 €)		Scenario 1 (capital expenditure 1,000,000 €)		Scenario 2 (capital expenditure 100,000 €)	
Country in which the fund is located: Italy		Distribution	Retention	Distribution	Retention	Distribution	Retention	Distribution	Retention
Fund investing domestically	Stocks	18.91 %	17.02 %	18.91 %	17.02 %	10.34 %	17.94 %	6.56 %	15.05 %
	Bonds	19.61 %	18.23 %	19.61 %	18.23 %	22.88 %	18.76 %	19.55 %	15.33 %

Analysis

Where an Italian taxpayer buys units in funds investing domestically he is subject to different tax burdens depending on the constellation concerned. In scenarios 1 and 2 the tax burdens differ only with regard to units in business property. There are no differences between taxation of equity and bond funds. The different burden figures therefore arise as a result of the model assumptions.

Distributions and capital gains from fund shares held in business property are subject to income tax assessment and are therefore taxed at the individual progressive tax rate. As a consequence, in corresponding cases the tax burden in scenario 2 is lower than that in scenario 1.

Although the investor may credit taxes withheld at fund level and only part of distributed dividend income is taxable, due to the fact that the income is subject to the progressive tax rate, the tax burden of an investor holding his units in business property is not, per se, lower than in the case of units held in private property; the tax burden may even exceed that of investors holding units in private property. The advantage of distributing equity funds compared to retaining equity funds arises from the fact that in case of distribution only 49.72 % of the earnings are taxable.

At fund level, there are no differences between taxation of equity funds and funds investing in bonds. Equity funds, however, appear to be advantageous due to the higher proportion of unrealized capital gains.

3.2.6 Japan

3.2.6.1 Qualitative Description
Short Description of the Tax System

Contract type Japanese Securities and Investment Trusts (SIT) of the contract type are not legal entities and therefore face no individual corporate taxation at fund level. Nevertheless, SITs of the contract type are not fully transparent. Thus, distributions qualify as either interest (bond fund) or as dividends (share and mixed fund), irrespective of the underlying assets. In general, Japan applies a withholding tax at asset level which is not levied if certain conditions are met.

Distributed earnings are subject to taxation at investor level in the form of withholding tax only, unless comprehensive taxation is filed. Such withholding tax amounts to up to 20 % for a domestic investor depending on the type of fund. Retained earnings are not normally subject to taxation. Profits from the disposal of units in bond funds are tax exempt. Profits from the disposal of units in equity and mixed funds face a two-level tax rate of up to 20 % depending on the type of fund.

Foreign investors need to be aware of some particular aspects affecting withholding taxes.
Company type Japanese SITs of the company type are individual legal entities and hence subject to corporate income tax. Under certain conditions, distributions may be deductible. In general, Japan applies a withholding tax at asset level which is not levied if certain conditions are met. Distributed earnings are subject to taxation at investor level in the form of withholding tax only, unless comprehensive taxation is filed. Dividend income is subject to withholding tax up to 20 % for a domestic investor depending on the type of fund. Retained earnings are not normally subject to taxation. Profits from the disposal of units face a two-level tax rate of up to 20 %.

Again, foreign investors need to be aware of some particular aspects affecting withholding taxes.

Basic Information and Sources of Law Concerning the Taxation of Funds

Description and basic characteristics	• SIT (Securities Investment Trust):
	  – Contract type.
	  – Company type: in practice only for REITS.
	• Nin-i-kumiai, a specific venture capital fund.

Investment supervision	Financial Services Agency (FSA).

Sources of law	• SIT (Securities Investment Trust):
	  – The Act on Investment Trust and Investment Corporation (May 31, 2000) as amended.
	  – The Trust Law (December 15, 2006).
	• Nin-i-kumiai, a specific venture capital fund:
	  – Civil law (April 27, 1896).
	  – Limited Partnership Act for Investment (June 3, 1998).

Taxation at Fund Level

Method of income taxation (tax rate)	*Contract type:*
	• Generally no corporate tax liability.
	• But entity not fully transparent for tax purposes.
	Company type:
	• Generally separate corporate tax liability (approximately 42 %).
	• Distributions are generally not deductible as operating costs.
	• Under the following requirements, distributions may be deductible:
	  – Registration with the Ministry. Compliance with certain requirements concerning issue, management and the holding of fund units.
	  – The corporation fulfills one of the following requirements: (1) At the establishment, the total value of the issued fund units (public offering) must be 100 million yen or more; or (2) The issued fund units are owned by 50 persons or more or owned solely by qualified institutional investors at the end of the accounting period.
	  – Fund units must be primarily offered in Japan.
	  – A minimum 90 % of the available profit for distributions is distributed.
	  – No fund qualification as "Family Company" at the end of the tax year[a].
	  – The corporation does not own 50 % or more of issued stocks of another corporation.
	  – Other conditions.

(continued)

Consideration of losses	*Contract type:* No tax levied at fund level. *Company type:* Loss can be carried forward for the subsequent 7 years in the same manner as normal corporate enterprises.
Treaty Access of the fund vehicle	*Japanese company type:* General treaty access. Normally a residency certificate is required. *Japanese contract type:* Generally no treaty access. *Foreign funds:* Generally no treaty access.
Crediting of withholding taxes levied at asset level	*Japanese company type:* Withholding tax is not levied under certain conditions. If levied, creditable or refundable against corporate income tax. *Contract type:* Withholding tax is not levied if certain administrative conditions are met.
Distribution obligation for taxation reasons	No.

Withholding tax (tax rate)	*Contract type:*
	• Bond investment trust[b]:
	  – 20 %[c] on distribution.
	• Stock investment trust:
	  – 20 % on distribution from privately offered stock investment trust.
	  – 10 %[d] (20 %[c] on or after January 1, 2012) on distribution from publicly offered stock investment trust.
	Company type:
	  – In principle, 20 % on dividends.
	  – Reduced withholding tax of 10 %[d] (20 %[c] on or after January 1, 2012) on dividends from listed funds or publicly offered investment trusts.

Specific characteristics of foreign assets/investors	*Foreign assets:*
	Crediting of foreign withholding taxes withheld at asset level:
	• *Contract type:* Withholding taxes can be credited against the Japanese withholding tax imposed on distributions at the Japanese fund level under certain conditions.
	• *Company type:* The crediting of tax paid follows the rules applying to normal corporate enterprises.
	Foreign investors:
	Only withholding tax is imposed. The tax rates are as follows:
	Contract type:
	• Bond investment trust:
	  – 15 %[e] on distribution.
	• Stock investment trust:
	  – 20 % on distribution from privately offered stock investment trust.

(continued)

– 7 %[f] (15 %[e] on or after January 1, 2012) on distribution from publicly offered stock investment trust.
Company type:
– In principle, 20 % on dividends.
– Reduced withholding tax of 7 % (15 % on or after January 1, 2012) on dividends from publicly offered stock investment trust.
The above tax rates may be reduced under the relevant treaty.

[a]Family companies are those whose shares are owned more than 50 % by the 1 largest shareholder
[b]Bond investment trust is defined as securities investment trust which has the purpose of investing exclusively in bonds and not in equities
[c]15 % income tax and 5 % inhabitant tax
[d]7 % income tax and 3 % inhabitant tax
[e]15 % income tax
[f]7 % income tax

Taxation at Investor Level

Distributed interest/dividends (tax rate)	• *Privately offered stock investment trust:* In addition to the withholding tax, distributions are subject to comprehensive taxation (15 %, 20 %, 30 %, 33 %, 43 %, 50 %)[a]. • *Publicly offered stock investment trust:* Withholding tax only. • *Bond investment trust:* Withholding tax only.
Distributed capital gains (tax rate)	• *Privately offered stock investment trust:* In addition to the withholding tax, distributions are subject to comprehensive taxation (15 %, 20 %, 30 %, 33 %, 43 %, 50 %)[a]. • *Publicly offered stock investment trust:* Withholding tax only. • *Bond investment trust:* Withholding tax only.
Accumulated interest/dividends (tax rate)	Not taxable until paid to investors as distributions
Accumulated capital gains (tax rate)	Not taxable until paid to investors as distributions
Consideration of the withholding taxes withheld at the domestic asset level	N/A.
Consideration of the withholding taxes withheld at the foreign asset level	Where the fund is a partnership vehicle treated as pass-through for Japanese tax purposes, the investor is treated as directly holding the underlying assets and any withholding taxes imposed on asset level should be creditable/refundable. Where the fund is a corporate vehicle, no credit (nor refund/deduction) should be available for withholding taxes imposed on asset level.
Consideration of the withholding taxes withheld at the domestic fund level	In principle, withholding tax imposed on distributions is creditable against investor's income tax.
Consideration of the withholding taxes withheld at foreign fund level	In principle, withholding tax imposed on distributions is creditable against investor's income tax.

(continued)

3.2 Tabular Representation

Special characteristics for foreign funds	• For foreign funds, withholding tax is withheld by the Japanese paying agent if the distributions are paid through the agent. • Accumulated income may be subject to taxation in accordance with the Japanese CFC guidelines.
Profit from the disposal (sale) of fund units (tax rate)	*Contract type:* • Bond investment trust: Profits from disposal are not taxable. • Stock investment trust: Profits from disposal are taxable at 20 %[b] by separate assessment taxation. Reduced at 10 %[c] for publicly offered stock investment trust until December 31, 2011 (thereafter 20 %). *Company type:* • Profits from disposal are taxable at 20 %[b] by separate assessment taxation. Reduced to 10 %[c] for listed stock investment trust until December 31, 2011 (thereafter 20 %).

[a]Basis for taxation: ¥ 0—¥ 1,950; ¥ 1,951—¥ 3,300; ¥ 3,301—¥ 6,950; ¥ 6,951—¥ 9,000; ¥ 9,001—¥ 18,000; over ¥ 18,000
[b]15 % income tax and 5 % inhabitant tax
[c]7 % income tax and 3 % inhabitant tax

3.2.6.2 Quantitative Comparison of Tax Burden for a Japanese Investor

		Fund units in private property			
		Scenario 1 (capital expenditure 1,000,000 €)		Scenario 2 (capital expenditure 100,000 €)	
Country in which the fund is located: Japan		Distribution	Retention	Distribution	Retention
Fund investing domestically (contract type)	Stocks	9.40 %	8.37 %	9.40 %	8.37 %
	Bonds	15.67 %	0.00 %	15.67 %	0.00 %
Fund investing domestically (company type)	Stocks	9.40 %	33.66 %	9.40 %	33.66 %
	Bonds	7.83 %	32.90 %	7.83 %	32.90 %

Analysis

In general, there are no differences between scenario 1 and scenario 2. This is due to the application of a flat rate taxation in all cases under consideration.

Contract type The two scenarios can lead to substantial differences in tax burden for the different case constellations. Compared to the distribution alternative, investment in a cumulative equity fund (retention alternative) gives rise to a slight advantage in terms of tax burden resulting from a positive time effect since retained earnings are taxed neither at investor nor at fund level. This means that in the case of the cumulative equity fund the tax burden results exclusively from the taxation of capital gains upon sale of the fund units.

(continued)

Distributions from bond funds are taxed at a higher rate (20 %) than those from equity funds (10 %). At the same time any gain from the disposal of fund units stays tax-free. Consequently, the tax differential between the distribution and retention alternative is significantly larger than in the case of equity funds.

Company type As far as funds of the company type are concerned, the investment in a distributing fund is substantially more advantageous than the investment in a growth fund. This is caused by the corporate tax liability on retained income.

In contrast to funds of the contract type, funds of the company type are obliged to withhold a uniform 10 % tax rate on distributed dividends as well as on distributed interest. Therefore the differences in the tax burdens between equity and bond funds shown in the table result from the model assumptions.

3.2.7 Luxembourg

3.2.7.1 Qualitative Description
Short Description of the Tax System

In principle, investments in a SICAF, SICAV or a FCP are taxed identically apart from small exceptions.

SICAF, SICAV Investment Companies in the form of a SICAF or SICAV represent non-transparent entities which are however subjected to no individual (corporate) tax liability. There is no withholding tax on any distribution made by the Fund whatever the residency, whatever the quality of the investors, unless the EU Savings Directive may apply (see above). For capital gains, it is dependent on the holding period and shareholding level.

The distributed profits at investor level are taxable. Distributed interest and dividends count as dividends and are subjected to the individual progressive income tax rate up to 38.95 %. The taxation of distributed capital gains depends on the holding period and shareholding. The earnings, if necessary, face the progressive tax rate up to 38.95 %. Whereas, retained earnings are not taxable. The disposal or return of fund units concerning Luxembourg investors is subjected to the individual progressive income tax rate up to 38.95 % if the holding period is shorter than 6 months. For foreign investors, the respective earnings are tax free.

FCP FCPs are not subjected to taxation as transparent units. At source taxation at fund level depends on whether Luxembourg or foreign investors are involved. There is no withholding tax on any distribution made by the fund whatever the residency, whatever the quality of the investors, unless the EU Savings Directive may apply (see above). For capital gains, it is dependent on the holding period and shareholding amount.

Please note that under certain conditions, DTT between country of investments and country of investors may apply.

The distributed profits at investor level are taxable. The classification of earnings conforms to the underlying assets. Distributed interest and dividends are subjected to the individual progressive income tax rate up to 38.95 %. The taxation of distributed capital gains depends on the holding period and the shareholding. The earnings, if necessary, face the progressive tax rate up to

(continued)

38.95 %. Retained earnings are taxable. The disposal or return of fund units concerning Luxembourg investors is subjected to the individual progressive income tax rate up to 38.95 % if the holding period is shorter than 6 months. For foreign investors, the respective earnings are tax free.

Basic Information and Sources of Law Concerning the Taxation of Funds

Description and basic characteristics	• SICAF: Investment Company with fixed capital. • SICAV: Investment Company with variable capital. • FCP: Investment Company (unit trust). • Available legal forms for SICAF, SICAV and FCP: – Public limited company (S.A.)[a]. – Private limited liability company (S.a.r.l.)[b]. – Partnership limited by shares (S.C.A.)[b]. – Cooperative organized as an S.A.[b]. • Most common form: FCP and SICAV.
Investment supervision	Commission de Surveillance du Secteur Financier (CSSF)
Sources of law	• No separate investment tax law. • Guidelines for the tax treatment of earnings from investment funds are found in the following sources: – The 2002 Law on UCIs[c]. – The 2007 Law on SIFs[d]. – The Law on Commercial Companies[e]. – The Law on the Financial Sector[f]. – The Law on the EU Savings Directive[g]. – The Law on Markets in Financial Instruments[h]. – The Circulars 91/75, 02/77, 02/80, 02/81, 03/87, 03/88, 03/97, 03/108, 03/122, etc.

[a]According to the law from December 20, 2002
[b]According to the law from February 13, 2007
[c]Last changed on December 20, 2002
[d]Last changed on February 13, 2007
[e]Last changed on August 10, 1915
[f]Last changed on April 5, 1993
[g]Last changed on June 20, 2005
[h]Last changed on July 13, 2007

Taxation at Fund Level

Method of income taxation (tax rate)	*SICAF, SICAV:* Non-transparent entities. No individual income taxation.[a] *FCP:* No individual income taxation (transparent entity).[a]
Consideration of losses	No.

(continued)

Treaty access of the fund vehicle	*Luxembourg Funds:* • In principle: Treaty access is regularly available, if the fund gives a residency certificate from the Luxembourg Fiscal Authority to the contract country, with the following information: – Fund is incorporated in Luxembourg. – Management and the Controlling Authority are in Luxembourg. • Luxembourg SICAF/SICAV: – In principle yes. – Some states reject the Luxembourg SICAVs treaty access. – Access should be granted to 28 double tax treaties. • Luxembourg FCP: – In principle no treaty access. – In some individual cases, treaty access is possible. *Foreign funds:* • Generally no treaty access. • Individual case by case decision.
Crediting of withholding taxes withheld at asset level	N/A.
Distribution obligation for taxation reasons	No.
Withholding tax (tax rate) upon distribution	• In principle no. • Yes, under the following conditions according to the interest tax guidelines: – For the part of the distribution which stems from the debt claims, if more than 15 % of the sub fund's assets stem from debt receivables. – For the part of the capital gains which stem from the debt claims, if more than 40 % of the relevant sub fund's assets are debt receivables. Please note that the redemption threshold will decrease to 25 % as from January 1, 2011. – Withholding tax rate: 20 % (until June 30, 2011), 35 % (from July 1, 2011).
Specific characteristics of foreign assets/investors	*Foreign assets:* No specific features. *Foreign investors:* • Distributed interest and dividends: – In principle not taxable. – In accordance with the interest tax guidelines, distributions that qualify as interest payments from a Luxembourg paying agent to an investor from another EU state can be subject to withholding tax (20 % until June 30, 2011, 35 % from July 1, 2011).

(continued)

3.2 Tabular Representation

- With distributed capital gains, the tax liability depends on the holding period and the shareholding, unless a Double Tax Treaty (DTT) may apply:
  - Holding period longer than 6 months and shareholding[b] of maximum 10 % at some point within the last 5 years before the disposal: no withholding tax or any other tax in Luxembourg
  - Holding period less than 6 months and shareholding[b] of maximum 10 % at some point within the last 5 years before the disposal: no withholding tax or any other tax in Luxembourg
  - Holding period longer than 6 months and shareholding[b] higher than 10 % at some point within the last 5 years before the disposal: in principle not taxable, exception with transfer of residence[c] (maximum 38.95 % for Luxembourg individuals).
  - Holding shorter than 6 months and shareholding[b] higher than 10 % at some point within the last 5 years before the disposal: the capital gains are subjected to a progressive income tax rate like domestic earnings (maximum 38.95 %).
- Disposal/return of fund units is in principle not taxable; in accordance with interest tax guidelines, distributions from a Luxembourg paying agent that qualify as interest payments to an investor from another EU state, can be subject to withholding tax (20 % until June 30, 2011, 35 % from July 1, 2011).
- No possibility of consideration of withholding taxes.

[a]But tax liability concerning a subscription tax of 0.05 % (0.01 % for funds which invest in money market instruments and cash deposits in banks)
[b]Direct or indirect shareholding
[c]Capital gains are taxable under the following conditions: Foreign investor was resident in Luxembourg in the past for a minimum of 15 years and the residency was ended in the last 5 years before the disposal of fund units

Taxation at Investor Level

Distributed interest/dividends (tax rate)	*SICAF, SICAV:* Taxable. Earnings qualify as dividends and are subjected to the individual progressive income tax rate (maximum 38.95 %[a]). *FCP:* Taxable. Classification of earnings conforms to the underlying assets. Individual progressive income tax rate applies (maximum 38.95 %[a]).
Distributed capital gains (tax rate)	*SICAF, SICAV:* Earnings qualify as dividends. Tax liability dependent on holding period, unless a DTT may apply:

(continued)

	• Holding period longer than 6 months: tax free. • Holding period shorter than 6 months: Taxable. Individual progressive income tax rate applies (maximum 38.95 %[b] for Luxembourg individuals). *FCP:* Classification of earnings conforms to the underlying assets. Tax liability otherwise identical to SICAF/SICAV.
Accumulated interest/dividends (tax rate)	*SICAF, SICAV:* Not taxable. *FCP:* Taxable. See "Distributed interest/dividends (tax rate)" above.
Accumulated capital gains (tax rate)	*SICAF, SICAV:* Not taxable. *FCP:* Taxable. See "Distributed capital gains (tax rate)" above.
Consideration of withholding taxes withheld at the domestic asset level	N/A.
Consideration of withholding taxes withheld at the foreign asset level	*SICAF, SICAV:* No. *FCP:* • Reduction of withholding tax under the DTT between the country of investment and country of investor if both countries consider the FCP to be transparent.
Consideration of the withholding taxes withheld at the domestic fund level	N/A.

Consideration of the withholding taxes withheld at the foreign fund level	• Foreign funds are non-transparent:
	  – No.
	• Foreign funds are transparent:
	  – Yes, in theory, crediting against Luxembourg earnings which are equivalent to the foreign earnings. Practically seems not possible.

Special characteristics of the foreign funds	Disposal/redemption of fund units is not taxable.
Profit from the disposal of fund units (tax rate)	Tax liability dependent on holding period, unless a DTT may apply: • Holding period longer than 6 months: tax free. • Holding period shorter than 6 months: Disposal/redemption is subject to the individual income tax rate (maximum 38.95 %[c] for individuals).

[a]Additionally, a special "dependency contribution" of 1.4 % of the gross pay for Luxembourg workers
[b]Certain deductions can be made
[c]Top tax rate begins with an income of more than 81,200 €

3.2.7.2 Quantitative Comparison of Tax Burden for a Luxembourgish Investor

Country in which the fund is located: Luxembourg		Fund units in private property			
		Scenario 1 (capital expenditure 1,000,000 €)		Scenario 2 (capital expenditure 100,000 €)	
		Distribution	Retention	Distribution	Retention
Fund investing domestically (FCP)	Stocks	22.27 %	22.66 %	15.44 %	15.77 %
	Bonds	26.29 %	26.74 %	18.21 %	18.53 %
Fund investing domestically (SICAV)	Stocks	22.27 %	0.51 %	15.44 %	0.51 %
	Bonds	26.29 %	0.88 %	18.21 %	0.88 %

Analysis

FCP Where a Luxembourg taxpayer invests in a "*Fonds Commun de Placement*" (FCP), the several case constellations of both scenarios offer slight differences between the corresponding tax burdens.

The findings demonstrate that the growth fund is slightly disadvantageous for the investor. This is due to the principle of tax transparency according to which the investor is liable to income tax on the income generated by the fund, irrespective of whether the income is actually distributed.

In scenario 2 the tax burden upon distribution is lower, due to the progressive tax rates.

SICAV As far as the distribution alternative is considered, the tax burdens on investments in a "*Société d'Investissement à Capital Variable*" (SICAV) are equal to those in the FCP case since there are no differences between the taxation concepts.

Shareholders in a SICAV, however, are not liable to tax on income accrued to the fund in case of retention. Moreover, gains from the disposal or redemption of the fund units are exempt from income tax. Therefore, the only tax burden that arises in case of an accumulating SICAV lies in the annual subscription tax of 0.05 % on the net asset value of the fund.

3.2.8 Netherlands

3.2.8.1 Qualitative Description
Short Description of the Tax System

In the Netherlands UCITS conforming investment funds may be launched in the form of investment companies or as contractual funds. Investment companies are generally subject to corporate income tax. Contractual funds are mostly structured as tax transparent.

However, under certain conditions a Naamloze vennootschap (Public limited company "N.V."), Besloten vennootschap (Limited company "B.V."), non-transparent Fonds voor Gemene Rekening (Fund for joint account managed by a management company "FGR") can opt for the status of fiscale beleggingsinstelling ("FBI"). Under certain conditions also foreign entities are eligible to claim the FBI regime. FBI is taxed at a corporate income tax ("CIT") rate of 0 %.

Furthermore, a N.V. and a FGR may under certain conditions claim the status of vrijgestelde beleggingsinstelling ("VBI"), which is exempt from CIT purposes.

(continued)

Taxation at fund level:
VBI The VBI is tax exempt for CIT purposes. Being qualified investment institutions, VBI are not liable to withholding tax at asset level. There is no distribution obligation of the earned income. At fund level there is no further withholding tax.

A VBI may invest in financial instruments ("transferable securities") only (not directly in real estate situated in the Netherlands). The activities of a VBI must consist exclusively of portfolio investments. No investor restrictions (minimum two investors required).

No regulatory supervision if amount of single participation is at least €50,000.

FBI Investment funds in the form of FBIs are subject to a corporate income tax rate of 0 %. Capital gains on investment can be provided for in a reinvestment reserve, to prevent that part of the fund's taxable income from being liable to withholding taxes in the course of an actual distribution or a notional minimum distribution. Regarding (deemed) distributed dividend income withholding taxes at a rate of 15 % (rate may be reduced by a DTT) are withheld on behalf of the investor at fund level. Withholding taxes at asset level can be deducted from the withholding taxes at fund level. Interest income can be paid out gross.

The statutory purpose and actual activities of the entity must consist exclusively of passive investments. The FBI is however allowed to hold shares in a subsidiary the main statutory and actual goal of which is property development for the benefit of the FBI.

There is an obligation to distribute earned income to the investors within 8 months of the end of the tax year. The distribution obligation does not apply to capital gains, if opted for the reinvestment reserve ("HBR").

To apply the FBI regime specific shareholder requirements have to be met. These shareholder requirements can be distinguished in strict and relaxed shareholder requirements. If the strict shareholder requirements apply, at least 75 % of the share capital must be held by individuals, entities not subject to corporate income tax or regulated FBIs. Furthermore, one individual may not hold 5 % or more in the FBI. If the more relaxed shareholder requirements apply, one individual may not hold a share of 25 % or more and less than 45 % of the share capital may be held by an entity or group of related entities subject to CIT. Resident shareholders may not hold indirectly 25 % or more of the shares in a FBI through non-resident entities.

No regulatory supervision if amount of single participation is at least 50,000 €.

FGR/CV No taxation at fund level, as tax transparent. The income is allocated to the investors in the fund.

No regulatory supervision if amount of single participation is at least 50,000 €.

Taxation at investor level (assuming that the investors hold a shareholding of less than 5 % in the fund):
The taxation of the investor is not based on the actual income. This applies independent of the use of the income (distribution, accumulation) and of the form of the fund (VBI, FBI). 4 % of the average market value of the underlying assets is subject to the taxation at a rate of 30 %, so in essence the tax burden is 1.2 %.[a] The withholding tax at fund level may be credited at investor level.

Dutch funds—Specifics for foreign assets and/or investors:
VBI Because the VBI is personally tax exempt for CIT purposes, it does not have treaty access. Foreign withholding taxes at asset level may not be considered at fund level. The investors in a VBI may also not consider the foreign withholding taxes at asset level. Thus in this case a foreign withholding taxation becomes unavoidable.

(continued)

FBI The FBI is taxed at a rate of 0 %, but is not personally tax exempt for CIT purposes. Therefore a FBI has access to treaty relief, based on which foreign withholding taxes on dividends and interest may be reduced. The amount of taxes withheld on dividends and interest at foreign level in principle reduces the withholding tax on dividends (there is no interest withholding tax in the Netherlands) from FBI to the foreign investors in the FBI. The reduction depends on the composition of the investors. No reduction if and to the extent that the foreign investor in the FBI is not entitled to reduction of the withholding tax based on a DTT.

Investor—Specific characteristics of foreign assets and funds:
Withholding taxes that are levied at the level of the foreign fund can be credited by the investor, as long as the funds location is a DTT-country or developing country (list).

[a]The average market value is determined from the market value at the beginning and at the end of the tax year

Basic Information and Sources of Law Concerning the Taxation of Funds

Description and basic characteristics	• Funds for joint account (FGR) structured as tax transparent. • Limited Partnership (CV) structured as tax transparent. • Tax exempt investment institution, "vrijgestelde beleggingsinstelling" (VBI). • Investment institution "fiscale beleggingsinstelling" (FBI).
Investment supervision	Autoriteit Financiële Markten (AFM).
Sources of law	• No separate investment tax act. • Regulations for the tax treatment of income from investment funds are found in the following sources: – The Financial Supervision Act; ("Wet financieel toezicht"—Wft)[a]. – The Further Regulations on the Market Conduct Supervision of Collective Investment Schemes[a]. – The Decree of 23 July 2005, containing provisions in implementation of the Act on the Supervision of Collective Investment Schemes[a]. – Corporate Income Tax Act 1969. – Income Tax Act 2001.

[a]Last amended 2007

Taxation at Fund Level

Method of income taxation (tax rate)	*VBI:* Corporate income tax exempt. *FBI:* Ordinary income taxed at a rate of 0 %, capital gains tax exempt if opted for reinvestment reserve ("HBR"), refer to the general outline below. *FGR/CV:* None, tax transparent.
Consideration of losses	*VBI:* No consideration at fund level. *FBI:* Normal loss utilization rules apply to FBI (carry-forward period: 9 years; carry-back period: 1 year). *FGR/CV:* N/A.

(continued)

Treaty access of the fund vehicle	*VBI:* No treaty access. *FBI:* Generally has treaty access. *FGR/CV:* No treaty access. *Treaty access of foreign vehicles:* • Fund should have a corporate nature and be non tax exempt. • Residence certificate of the fund's country.
Crediting of withholding taxes withheld at asset level	*VBI:* N/A. *FBI:* No, but reduction of withholding tax upon distributions by FBI contribution may apply. *FGR/CV:* No.
Distribution obligation for taxation reasons	*VBI:* No. *FBI:* Yes, distribution within 8 months of the end of the tax year. However, (broadly) only for ordinary income. *FGR/CV:* No.
Dividend withholding tax (15 %) (No withholding tax on interest in the Netherlands).	*VBI:* No. *FBI:* Yes (15 %) but may be reduced based on double tax treaty ("DTT"). The amount of dividend withholding tax to be paid to the tax authorities may be reduced by withholding taxes on income received by FBI. *FGR/CV:* No.
Specific characteristics of foreign assets/investors	*VBI:* Foreign assets: • No consideration of withholding taxes withheld at the foreign asset level, as no access to DTT. Investments restricted to financial instruments ("transferable securities"). Foreign investors: • No investor restrictions (minimum two investors required). *FBI:* Foreign assets: • Deduction of withholding tax withheld at the foreign asset level from the withholding tax of the fund. • No limit on eligible assets, as long as they are passive investments. Foreign investors: • Severe shareholder requirements apply; refer to the general outline below. • Reduction of withholding tax on distribution to foreign investor in the FBI depends on the composition of the investors. *FGR/CV:* No specific characteristics of foreign investors/assets.

3.2 Tabular Representation

Taxation at Investor Level

Distributed interest/dividends (30 %)	Distributed interest/dividends are taxed in hands of resident investor (taxation of average market value), refer to general outline below.
Distributed capital gains (30 %)	Distributed capital gains are taxed in hands of resident investor (taxation of average market value), refer to general outline below.
Accumulated interest/dividends (30 %)	Accumulated interest/dividends are taxed in hands of resident investor (taxation of average market value), refer to general outline below.
Accumulated capital gains (30 %)	Accumulated capital gains are taxed in hands of resident investor (taxation of average market value), refer to general outline below.
Consideration of the withholding taxes withheld at the domestic asset level	*VBI:* N/A *FBI:* No. *FGR/CV:* Yes (credit), as tax transparent.
Consideration of the withholding taxes withheld at foreign asset level	If the fund is considered as a non-transparent entity, the investor cannot credit, refund or deduct withholding tax which is withheld on income received by the fund.
Consideration of the withholding taxes withheld at the domestic fund level	*VBI:* N/A. *FBI:* Yes (credit/refund). *FGR/CV:* N/A.
Consideration of the withholding taxes withheld at the foreign fund level	In principle, the local investor can deduct the withholding tax from its personal income tax payable. The deductible amount cannot exceed the foreign withholding tax or the pro-rata part of the Dutch personal income tax due over the foreign dividend income. If a double tax treaty is applicable, it should be assessed how the foreign withholding tax is treated for Dutch personal income tax purposes.
Special characteristics of the foreign funds	• No treaty access if the fund is regarded as transparent for tax purposes. Consideration of withholding taxes at asset level depends on the DTT. • Three-country-case: In case the fund does not qualify from the Dutch perspective as tax transparent, the foreign fund should pursue the consideration of the withholding taxes according to the law of this country.
Profit from the disposal of fund units (30 %)	*VBI, FBI:* Not taxable. *FGR/CV:* Capital gains from the disposal are not in themselves taxable. However, tax liability is incurred indirectly as a (proportionate) disposal of the fund's assets is deemed when fund units are disposed of.

3.2.8.2 Quantitative Comparison of Tax Burden for a Dutch Investor[1]

		Fund units in private property			
		Scenario 1 (capital expenditure 1,000,000 €)		Scenario 2 (capital expenditure 100,000 €)	
Country in which the fund is located: Netherlands		Distribution	Retention	Distribution	Retention
Fund investing domestically	Stocks	16.20 %	16.20 %	16.20 %	16.20 %
	Bonds	20.60 %	20.60 %	20.60 %	20.60 %

Analysis

FBI and VBI In principle, taxation of equity and bond funds is identical, but in case of retention the outcome is different due to the definitive withholding of tax on domestic dividends accruing to the fund.

Despite this fundamentally identical taxation of bond and equity funds, overall the equity fund brings greater return in all case constellations. The reason lies in the taxation of the deemed profit. Hence the effective tax burden is affected substantially by the difference between deemed and real returns. The effective tax burden of the investor will decrease or increase depending on the spread between deemed and real returns.

The equity fund in our case study shows an overall return amounting to 10.78 %, while the bond fund has an overall return of 6.00 %. Thus the investor's tax burden is clearly lower in the case of equity funds due to the amount of the deemed returns, which is as little as 4 %. Therefore the effective tax burden decreases with the fund's increasing success, whereas low-yield or loss-making fund structures can give rise to comparatively high tax burdens.

3.2.9 Poland

3.2.9.1 Qualitative Description
Short Description of the Tax System

Open- and closed-ended investment funds Investments in an open- or closed-ended investment fund are treated identically tax wise. Both fund types represent non-transparent entities and domestic investment funds are exempt from corporate income tax.

The distributed earnings, as well as income from redemption of fund units (participation units in open-ended fund and investment certificates in closed-ended funds), are in principle taxable at investor level. Tax of 19 % is withheld on distributions from the investment fund to investors. Income generated on sale of fund units to third parties is combined with income from disposal of securities (if any) and subject to 19 % tax settled annually by the investor (unless such disposal is made within business activities of the investor[a]).

[a]In this case, the income generated on disposal of investment certificates to third parties is declared in the tax return and taxed at 19 % as well.

---

[1] The calculations underlie the assumptions that the distributing funds are subject to the FBI system, while the retained funds are liable to the VBI system.

3.2 Tabular Representation

Basic Information and Sources of Law Concerning the Taxation of Funds

Description and basic characteristics	• Open-ended investment fund. • Closed-ended investment fund. • Legal form for both fund types: investment fund (a distinct type of entity having legal personality).
Investment supervision	• Komisja Nadzoru Finansowego (Financial Supervision Committee).
Sources of law	• Establishment and activities of the investment funds are regulated by The Act on Investment Funds[a]. • Guidelines for the tax treatment of earnings from investment assets are found in the following sources: – The Corporate Income Tax Act. – The Personal Income Tax Act.

[a]Last changed on October 31, 2009

Taxation at Fund Level

Method of income taxation (tax rate)	• Non-transparent entities. • Exempt from corporate income taxation.
Consideration of losses	No.
Treaty access of the fund vehicle	According to most double tax agreements, interest and dividends from foreign assets are subject to taxation in the source country (maximum 15 %). (Such income would not be subject to tax in Poland, since investment funds are exempt from income tax in Poland).
Crediting of withholding taxes withheld at asset level	N/A.
Distribution obligation for taxation reasons	No.
Withholding tax (tax rate)	Distributions made from the fund to investors are subject to withholding tax of 19 %.
Specific characteristics of foreign assets/investors	*Foreign assets:* • Domestic investment funds are exempt from Polish income tax regardless of the source or character of the income. • According to most double tax agreements, interest and dividends from foreign assets are subject to taxation in the source country (maximum 15 %). *Foreign investors:* Distribution of profits to foreign investors is subject to withholding tax of 19 %.

Taxation at Investor Level

Distributed interest/dividends (tax rate)	Distribution of profits derived by investment funds from interest/dividends/disposal of assets/any other source generally may take a form of distribution without redemption of the units in the fund. Such distributions are taxable as a separate source of revenue, i.e. such profit is not combined with income from other sources. Tax of 19 % is withheld at source (see above)

(continued)

Distributed capital gains (tax rate)	Distribution of profits derived by investment funds from interest/dividends/disposal of assets/any other source generally may take a form of distribution without redemption of the units in the fund. Such distributions are taxable as a separate source of revenue, i.e. such profit is not combined with income from other sources. Tax of 19 % is withheld at source (see above).
Accumulated interest/dividends (tax rate)	Not taxable.
Accumulated capital gains (tax rate)	Not taxable.
Consideration of the withholding taxes at the domestic asset level	N/A.
Consideration of the withholding taxes at the foreign asset level	If the fund is a tax resident in the country of its location, the investor should not be entitled to credit, refund or deduct the withholding tax deducted at the level of the asset. In the case of tax transparent funds, the possibility of crediting, refunding or deducting the withholding tax would require an in-depth analysis which should be made on a case by case basis.
Consideration of the withholding taxes at the domestic fund level	No.
Consideration of the withholding taxes at the foreign fund level	The investor would be entitled to credit the withholding tax. The credit amount would be limited to the amount of Polish tax due on the payment, if it would be paid in purely domestic/Polish situation. Other method of avoiding double taxation than the credit method may need to be applied, if there is a double tax treaty between the country of the fund (source) and Poland.
Special characteristics of the foreign funds	• Withholding tax for the distribution of dividends (19 %) and interest (20 %) from Polish assets on distributions to foreign funds, unless a relief from tax at source is applicable under double tax treaty[a], • In case the tax on income from participation in investment funds was not withheld at source (e.g. by foreign investment fund), Polish investor is obliged to account for this tax in his annual tax settlement. The investor is entitled to decrease the amount of tax due in Poland on distributions made from the fund to the investor by the amount of tax paid on such distribution abroad.
Profit from the disposal of fund units (tax rate)	Redemption of participation units[b] in open-ended investment funds, as well as redemption of investment certificates in closed-ended investment funds is subject to withholding tax of 19 %. The income generated on disposal of investment certificates to third parties is

(continued)

classified as income from sale of securities and subject to tax of 19 % remitted annually by the investor (unless such disposal is made within business activities of the investor[c]).

[a]According to the literal wording of the Polish CIT provisions, Polish investment funds are exempt from income taxation in Poland, whilst this exemption does not relate to the foreign funds running their activities in Poland. However, in our view such regulation is not in line with the EU directives, i.e. the exemption from CIT taxation should also be applicable in relation to these foreign funds, which fall under the EU regulations regarding Undertakings for Collective Investment in Transferable Securities
[b]Participation units in open-ended investment funds are generally not transferrable to third parties
[c]In this case, the income generated on disposal of investment certificates to third parties is declared in the tax return and taxed at 19 % as well

3.2.9.2 Quantitative Comparison of Tax Burden for a Polish Investor

		Fund units in private property			
		Scenario 1 (capital expenditure 1,000,000 €)		Scenario 2 (capital expenditure 100,000 €)	
Country in which the fund is located: Poland		Distribution	Retention	Distribution	Retention
Fund investing domestically	Stocks	17.96 %	16.14 %	17.96 %	16.14 %
	Bonds	18.62 %	17.30 %	18.62 %	17.30 %

Analysis

Open-ended and closed-ended funds For a Polish fund investor the tax burden varies between individual case constellations, but this is not dependent on the investment amount (scenario 1 and scenario 2) as the tax rates are not linked to income. The investor can gain an advantage by investing in a growth fund owing to the fact that retained earnings are tax free until sale or return of the units. In principle, no differences exist between equity and bond funds when it comes to taxation. So the differences arising here in tax burdens result from the model assumptions.

3.2.10 Switzerland

3.2.10.1 Qualitative Description
Short Description of the Tax System

SICAV and FCP Investments in a SICAV and an FCP are treated identically tax-wise. Both forms are treated as transparent entities without independent legal capacity. Therefore, they are not subject to independent income tax at fund level (with the exception of funds directly holding Swiss real estate). For earnings and profits derived as interest, dividend or other income (not including capital gains), 35 % withholding tax is retained at fund level, which the investors can credit. The fund can issue separate coupons for interest/dividend distributions/accumulations on the one hand and capital gains from assets on the other hand. In this case, only interest/dividends are subject to withholding tax.

(continued)

The taxing of earnings takes place at investor level. In so doing, one must distinguish between fund units held as private assets and as business assets. If the fund units are held as private assets, distributed interest and dividends are subject to tax at investor level. Accumulated interest and dividends are only taxed, if the fund distributes less than 70 % of its taxable earnings. Capital gains from the disposal or redemption of fund units are not taxable.

If the fund units are held as business assets, the complete distribution (interest, dividends, and capital gains) is subject to tax at investor level. Accumulated interest, dividends and capital gains are generally not taxable at investor level, even if the fund pays out less than 70 % of its earnings.

Basic Information and Sources of Law Concerning the Taxation of Funds

Description and basic characteristics	• Investment Company with variable capital (SICAV); legal form: public limited company, private limited company. • Investment fund (open investment scheme in contractual type; FCP) (most common form). • With both fund methods, a distinction in distributing and accumulating funds is made.
Investment supervision	Swiss financial market supervision (FINMA).
Sources of law	• No separate investment tax law. • Guidelines for the tax treatment of earnings from investment assets are found in: – Swiss Stamp Duty Law. – Swiss Direct Federal Tax Law. – Swiss Withholding Tax Law. – Swiss Withholding Tax Act Decree. – Swiss VAT Law. – Collective Investment Schemes Act. – Decree on the Collective Investment Scheme Act. – Circular Letter no. 24 and no. 25.

Taxation at Fund Level (Swiss Fund)

Method of income taxation (tax rate)	No income taxation (transparent entities), because no individual legal entity and tax liability. Other rules may apply in case the fund directly owns Swiss real estate.
Consideration of losses	No consideration.
Treaty access of the fund vehicle	Generally, no treaty access. Individual case decision subject to the respective double tax treaty.
Crediting of withholding taxes withheld at asset level	Yes, refund.
Distribution obligation for taxation reasons	No.
Withholding tax ("anticipatory tax", "*Verrechnungssteuer*") (tax rate)	*Funds distributing at least 70 % of taxable earnings ("Distributing Funds"):* • Fund distributions are subject to withholding tax (35 %). • Splitting up of the distributions into dividends/interest and capital gains through separate coupons is possible:

(continued)

3.2 Tabular Representation

	– No split: Withholding tax for all distributions (35 %). – Split: • Withholding tax for distributions from the dividends/interest account (35 %) • No withholding tax for distributions from the capital gains account *Funds distributing less than 70 % of taxable earnings ("Mixed Funds")/Funds accumulating 100 % of taxable earnings ("Growth Funds"):* • Fund distributions and accumulated earnings are subject to withholding tax (35 %) • Splitting up of the distributions/accumulating earnings into dividends/interest and capital gains through separate coupons is possible: – No split: Withholding tax for all distributions and accumulated earnings (35 %) – Split: • Withholding tax for distributions and accumulated earnings from the dividends/interest account (35 %) • No withholding tax for distributions/accumulated earnings from the capital gains account
Specific characteristics of foreign assets/investors	*Foreign assets of Swiss funds:* Swiss investors in Swiss funds possibly have access to withholding tax relief for dividends and/or interest in accordance with the double taxation treaty with certain countries. *Foreign investors in Swiss funds:* • Withholding tax on distributions (35 %). • Refund of withholding taxes according to the double tax treaty. – Exemption from withholding tax under the following conditions (Affidavit process): – Minimum 80 % of income stems from foreign sources or – There is a declaration from the custodian bank that the investor is not resident in Switzerland.

Taxation at Investor Level

Distributed interest/dividends (tax rate)	*Distributing fund:* Taxable (tax rate depends on the Canton, in which the tax payer resides). *Growth fund:* N/A. *Mixed fund:* Both distributed and retained part of interest/dividends is taxable (tax rate depends on the Canton, in which the tax payer resides).
Distributed capital gains (tax rate)	*Distributing fund:* • PA: Not taxable, if distributed with separate coupon. • BA: Taxable (tax rate depends on the Canton, in which the tax payer resides). *Growth fund:* N/A.

(continued)

	Mixed fund: • PA: Both distributed and retained part of capital gains is taxable (tax rate depends on the Canton, in which the tax payer resides), unless distributed with separate coupon or booked separately, respectively. • BA: Both distributed and retained part of capital gains is taxable (tax rate depends on the Canton, in which the tax payer resides).
Accumulated interest/dividends (tax rate)	*Distributing fund:* Not taxable. *Growth fund:* • PA: Taxable (tax rate depends on the Canton, in which the tax payer resides). • BA: Not taxable. *Mixed fund:* Both distributed and retained part of interest/dividends is taxable (tax rate depends on the Canton, in which the tax payer resides).
Accumulated capital gains (tax rate)	*Distributing fund:* Not taxable. *Growth fund:* • PA: Not taxable, if booked separately as capital gain. • BA: Not taxable. *Mixed fund:* • PA: Both distributed and retained part of capital gains is taxable (tax rate depends on the Canton, in which the tax payer resides), unless distributed with separate coupon or booked separately, respectively. • BA: Both distributed and retained part of capital gains is taxable (tax rate depends on the Canton, in which the tax payer resides).
Consideration of the withholding taxes at the domestic asset level	No.
Consideration of the withholding taxes at the foreign asset level	For Swiss investors only (general rule): • Dividends: Yes, crediting; refund according to double tax treaty. • Interest and capital gains from shares and bonds: No.
Consideration of the withholding taxes withheld at the domestic fund level	• PA: Yes, refund for dividends and interest. • BA: Yes, refund for dividends, interest and capital gains.
Consideration of the withholding taxes at the foreign fund level	Unilaterally no applicable option. Crediting and refund, if possible according to double tax agreement.
Special characteristics of the foreign funds	Foreign funds have a refund entitlement for withholding taxes withheld at asset level, under the requirements of the double tax treaty.
Profit from the disposal of fund units (tax rate)	• PA: Not taxable. • BA: Taxable. Yes. Basis for taxation is the difference between present value upon redemption and the acquisition costs (face value principle).

3.2.10.2 Quantitative Comparison of Tax Burden for a Swiss Investor[2]

Country in which the fund is located: Switzerland		Fund units in private property				Fund units in business property			
		Scenario 1 (capital expenditure 1,000,000 €)		Scenario 2 (capital expenditure 100,000 €)		Scenario 1 (capital expenditure 1,000,000 €)		Scenario 2 (capital expenditure 100,000 €)	
		Distribution	Retention	Distribution	Retention	Distribution	Retention	Distribution	Retention
Fund investing domestically	Stocks	5.10 %	5.17 %	3.13 %	3.14 %	18.91 %	22.81 %	11.19 %	15.64 %
	Bonds	5.10 %	5.17 %	3.13 %	3.14 %	18.91 %	22.81 %	11.19 %	15.64 %

Analysis

Private property Both in scenario 1 and 2 the tax burden on equity and bond funds is identical resulting from the equal treatment of interest and dividend income in all case constellations.

The comparison between scenario 1 and 2 shows a lower tax burden for scenario 2. The reasons for this is that due to the lower returns in scenario 2 (resulting from the model assumptions) the effect of progression arising with the direct federal tax has less impact on the investor's tax burden.

In case of cumulative funds an investor holding the fund units as private assets is liable to tax on his income irrespective of whether it is distributed or retained. In both cases, however, no income tax is due on capital gains realised at fund level, provided that (as it is assumed here) they are distributed with separate coupon or booked separately, respectively. The slight differences between the distribution and the retention alternative are reducible to time effects.

Business property As opposed to investors holding the fund units as private assets, share ownership in business assets entails an income tax liability of the investor not only on regular income but also on capital gains accrued to the fund. This leads to a broadening of the tax base and to intensification of the progression effect. Consequently, the resulting tax burdens are considerably higher than in the case of private property.

While in general investors holding the fund units in business property are not taxed on income accrued to the fund until its actual distribution, it must be kept in mind that the withholding taxation at fund level is also employed in case of retention. To make a credit or refund of these withholding taxes possible, the investor must recognize the income concerned for tax purposes. In our model, it is favourable for the investor to do so, that is to subject the retained regular income to tax in order to get a refund of excess taxes withheld at fund level.

3.2.11 Spain

3.2.11.1 Qualitative Description
Short Description of the Tax System

SICAV and Fondo de Inversión Investments in a SICAV and a Fondo de Inversión are treated identically tax wise under certain conditions. Both a SICAV (independent legal entity), as well as the non-legal entity distributing Fondo de Inversión are subject to Spanish corporate income tax.

Under the regulatory requirements described in the table, both fund vehicles qualify for reduced corporation tax (1 %).

(continued)

---

[2] The calculations are based on the following assumptions: The fund income is divided by separate coupons for interest, dividend income and capital gains from disposal of assets. The investor is subject to taxation in the community of Walchwill in the Canton Zug. The selection was made to choose firstly the Canton with the lowest tax rate. Afterwards the procedure was repeated to select a community with the lowest tax rate. For the determination of relevant variables in the calculations, the following sources were used: Eichenberger (2008), Eidgenössische Steuerverwaltung (2010), Finanzdirektion Steuerverwaltung Kanton Zug (2010) and Schweizerische Steuerkonferenz (2009a, b, c).

For distributed interest, dividends and capital gains, 19 % withholding taxes are withheld at fund level.

Paid out interest, dividends and capital gains are subjected to a 19 % tax rate.

Accumulated income is not subject to taxation.

The disposal of fund units is subject to 19 % taxation.

In case of individual Spanish residents, switches between funds can be tax free and not subject to 19 % withholding tax when certain requirements are met. Spanish Individuals Tax Law envisages that when the amount obtained as a consequence of the reimbursement or transmission of participations or shares in CIIs is applied to the acquisition of another shares or participations in CIIs no capital gain or loss arises and the new shares or participations will maintain the same acquisition date and value as the ones transferred or reimbursed, provided that certain requirements are met.

This deferral regime will not be applicable when, through any mean, the amount derived from the redemption or sale of shares or participations in the CII is made available to the tax payer. Deferral regime does not apply to Exchange Traded Funds regulated under article 49 of the Spanish Royal Decree 1309/2005.

Basic Information and Sources of Law Concerning the Taxation of Funds

Description and basic characteristics	• Investment Company with variable capital (SICAV) (most common form); legal form: public limited company, private limited company. • Investment fund (Fondo de Inversión).
Investment Supervision	Comision Nacional del Mercado de Valores (CNMV).
Sources of law	• No separate investment tax law. • Guidelines for the tax treatment of earnings from investment assets are found in: – Corporate Income Tax Law approved by Real Decreto Legislativo 4/2004. – Royal Decree 1777/2004 of Corporate Income Tax. – Personal Income Tax Law, Law 35/2006. – Law 35/2003[a]. – Law 24/1988[b]. – Royal Decree 1309/2005[c]. – CNMV guidelines[d]. – CNMV guideline 3/2006[e]. – CNMV guideline 1/2006[f].

[a]Approved on November 4, 2003
[b]Approved in 1988
[c]Approved on November 4, 2005
[d]Approved on June 13, 2007
[e]Approved on October 26, 2006
[f]Approved on May 3, 2006

Taxation at Fund Level

Method of income taxation (tax rate)	• A Spanish investment company or an investment fund meeting the minimum number of shareholders or participants provided by the CIIs Law qualify for a special tax system where the company or fund is subject to a 1 % corporate income tax rate. The minimum number of shareholders or participants is 100 (20 per compartment) as a general rule. Moreover, this minimum number of participants' requirement does not apply to funds which participant is exclusively another investment fund. • Spanish investment funds and companies cannot enjoy from any tax credits applicable to ordinary companies. However, to the extent they obtain income from foreign sources, they may enjoy from the credits or exemptions granted under the applicable double tax treaty. • Other investment companies or funds are subjected to the normal tax rules.
Consideration of losses	Tax losses can be offset in the following 15 years from their generation.
Treaty access of the fund vehicle	• Spanish funds are normally treaty entitled, because they are subjected to corporation tax. Guidelines regarding the treaty access of investment vehicles are contained in some DTTs, as for example with the USA, Korea, France and Germany. – Germany: Art. 10 part. 4 (Dividends). – France: Protocol 9. – USA: Protocol 7 (c) and (d) concerning article 10 (Dividends). • Foreign funds only have treaty access in Spain, if they are subjected to taxation in the state of residence. The treaty access is verified in Spain by possession of a valid state of residence certificate.
Crediting of withholding taxes withheld at asset level	Crediting of 1 %. The remaining 18 % (with dividends, interest) are refunded.
Distribution obligation for taxation reasons	No.
Withholding tax (tax rate)	As a general rule distributed dividends, interest[a], and capital gains obtained by the investment fund or company are subject to a 19 % withholding tax. Nevertheless, depending on types of income, specific situations, etc., several exemptions could apply.
Specific characteristics of foreign assets/investors	*Foreign investors:* • Dividend distributions are subject to a national withholding tax of 19 %, in case a double tax treaty/internal exception does not allow for a reduced tax rate (distributions) or exemption (capital gains). • Gains realized upon the sale or redemption of shares or participations of CII are subject to withholding tax. Please note that exemptions are applicable, e.g. listed investment funds, investors located in EU, etc.

[a]Interest on Spanish state borrowing is subjected with compliance to certain requirements and not to the at source tax deduction

Taxation at Investor Level

Distributed interest/dividends (tax rate)	Taxable. Dividends and interests are subject to 19 % taxation. No tax credit applicable.
Distributed capital gains (tax rate)	Taxable (19 %).
Accumulated interest/dividends (tax rate)	Not taxable.
Accumulated capital gains (tax rate)	Not taxable.
Consideration of withholding taxes withheld at the domestic asset level	No consideration.
Consideration of withholding taxes withheld at the foreign asset level	• Spanish investors can, according to national law or the double tax agreement, deduct withholding taxes for current income and capital gains, which were levied at the foreign asset level, for a foreign fund. According to national law, the deduction is limited to the smaller amount of the following: – Foreign withholding tax on dividends. – Average tax rate on foreign income shares. • Double tax agreement can allow for a differing credit system. • Foreign fund is resident in a "tax haven" ("black lists") (see also here special characteristics of foreign funds), the investor is resident in Spain: no deduction of foreign withholding taxes possible.
Consideration of withholding taxes withheld at the domestic fund level	Yes, credit/refund.
Consideration of withholding taxes at the foreign fund level	As regards any withholding tax in the foreign country where the fund is located, the provisions of the applicable treaty, if any, should be observed, as well as the application of the domestic tax credit for international double taxation which can be summarized as follows: When the taxpayer's income includes returns, earnings or capital gains obtained and taxed abroad, the lower of the following two amounts shall be deducted: • The actual amount paid abroad due to a tax of identical or analogous nature to the personal income tax or the non resident income tax on such returns, earnings or capital gains. • The result of applying the effective tax rate to the part of the net taxable base taxed abroad.
Special characteristics of the foreign funds	• UCITS-fund of an EU member state, which is registered in Spain: tax treatment as with Spanish UCITS-funds. • Taxation of funds in *"tax havens"* (*"black lists"*): The difference between the liquidation value of the fund shares at the end and the acquisition value at the beginning of the tax year is factored into the annual Spanish investor tax assessment basis. This difference is assessed as the lump sum of 15 % of the acquisition cost of the fund shares, if nothing else can be evidenced. Actual dividends are irrelevant for taxation. For the purposes of taxation of future capital

(continued)

	gains, distributions reduce the acquisition costs of the fund shares, whereas the underlying fund share value increase for taxation increases the acquisition costs. • Rest of world-fund: Case by case decision.
Profit from the disposal of fund units (tax rate)	Taxable. Capital gains realized on the sale or redemption of shares or participations are subject to 19 % withholding tax. Final taxation at the Spanish investor level is 19 %. In case of capital losses, individuals may only offset them against other capital gains. Capital losses in excess can be offset against capital gains of subsequent 4 years. Switches between funds can be tax free for Spanish resident individuals and not subject to 19 % withholding tax when certain requirements are met. Spanish Individuals Tax Law envisages that when the amount obtained as a consequence of the reimbursement or transmission of participations or shares in CIIs is applied to the acquisition of another shares or participations in CIIs no capital gain or loss arises and the new shares or participations will maintain the same acquisition date and value as the ones transferred or reimbursed, provided that certain requirements are met. This deferral regime will not be applicable when, through any mean, the amount derived from the redemption or sale of shares or participations in the CII is made available to the tax payer. Deferral regime does not apply to Exchange Traded Funds regulated under article 49 of the Spanish Royal Decree 1309/2005. Capital gains obtained on the sale or redemption of units in listed investment funds, regulated by article 49 Royal Decree 1309/2005, are exempt from withholding tax.

3.2.11.2 Quantitative Comparison of Tax Burden for a Spanish Investor

		Fund units in private property			
		Scenario 1 (capital expenditure 1,000,000 €)		Scenario 2 (capital expenditure 100,000 €)	
Country in which the fund is located: Spain		Distribution	Retention	Distribution	Retention
Fund investing domestically	Stocks	18.07 %	16.70 %	18.07 %	16.70 %
	Bonds	18.76 %	17.96 %	18.76 %	17.96 %

Analysis

For a Spanish fund investor the tax burden varies between individual case constellations, but this is not dependent on the investment amount (scenario 1 and scenario 2) as the tax rates are not linked to income.

For investments in growth funds, the Spanish investor can achieve a minor advantage from a temporary tax exemption at fund level, leading to a positive time effect until retained earnings are taxed at sale or return of fund units.

In principle, there is no difference, however, between the taxation of equity and bond funds. The differences in tax burden shown here result from the model assumptions regarding prospective returns, since in the case of an equity fund a larger proportion is treated as retained earnings.

3.2.12 USA

3.2.12.1 Qualitative Description
Short Description of the Tax System

RIC Generally, investments in a RIC are subject to taxation at fund level.[a] The accumulated gains (accrued gains from assets less distributions for investors) are liable to a 35 % corporate tax. If less than 98 % of the gains are distributed, there is an additional indirect tax for the retained gains in the amount of 4 %. In principle, a RIC is entitled to credit the foreign withholding taxes at asset level. Due to the wide effective tax exemption caused by distribution, there is the possibility to transfer the credit amount to the investors under certain requirements.

Distributed interest, dividends, short-term capital gains (maximum holding period of assets: 12 months) and distributed or retained capital gains (minimum holding period of assets and fund shares: 12 months) are liable to taxation at investor level. Thereby a progressive six-stage tax rate from 10 % to 35 % is applied for distributed interest, dividends, and short-term capital gains (holding period not more than 12 months). In contrast, the distributed or retained capital gains from assets, which are held longer than 12 months, are taxed at a progressive tax rate from 0 % to 15 %. The accrued taxes on retained capital gains are creditable against the tax liability of the according distributed profits. The investors are entitled to credit, if the transmission of the credit amount for the foreign withholding taxes is generated by the RIC. A great number of special regulations have to be respected for investments of American investors in foreign funds. Foreign funds are divided into three categories. There exist partly different tax consequences for those categories. Altogether, investments in foreign funds are subject to stricter tax regulations.

[a]Missing qualification as RIC: All earnings of the fund are subject to the common corporate tax rate in the amount of 15–35 %, independent of distribution or retention. If less than 98 % of the profits are distributed, there is an additional indirect tax amounting 4 % on the retained earnings

Basic Information and Sources of Law Concerning the Taxation of Funds

Description and basic characteristics	• RIC: Regulated Investment Company (most common form). Type of fund, which is comparable to the European UCITS-funds. In compliance with certain requirements, a fund qualifies as a RIC: – Diversification of investments. – Regulations concerning the nature and scope of the source of income. – Distribution of at least 90 % of the taxable interest and dividend income. A minimum distribution rate for taxable income from capital gains does not exist. – Legal forms: public limited company, private limited company. • Private Investment Company as subform of RIC: – Fund shares are not offered in public. – The economic ownership of fund shares presents not more than 100 investors during the term of the fund. – The target groups are particularly qualified large-scale investors (amount to be invested: $5 Mio.) and institutional investors (amount to be invested: $25 Mio.). They are subject to special reliefs regarding the regulation of the fund. – Sect. 3c par. 1 and 7 of the Investment Company Act.

(continued)

3.2 Tabular Representation

Investment supervision	Securities and Exchange Commission (SEC).
Sources of law	• No separate investment tax act. • Prescriptions for taxation of earnings from investment property can also be found in the following sources: – The Securities Act (1933). – The Securities Exchange Act (1934). – The Investment Company Act (1940). – The Investment Advisors Act (1940). – The Gramm-Leach-Bliley Act (1999). – The Sarbanes-Oxley Act (2002). – The Internal Revenue Code (1986) as amended.

Taxation at Fund Level

Method of income taxation (tax rate)	*RIC:* • Distributed dividends for the investors are deductable. • Retained earnings are taxable (35 %). • There is also a special indirect tax (4 % excise tax), if less than 98 % of the revenues are distributed. *Lack of qualification as RIC:* • All of the funds accruing interest, dividend income and earnings from the disposal of assets are subject to the usual corporation tax (from 15 % to 35 %), independent of distribution or retention. • There is also a special indirect tax (4 % excise tax), if less than 98 % of the income is distributed.
Consideration of losses	No consideration.
Treaty access of the fund vehicle	*US-RIC:* • Usually entitled to credit the foreign withholding taxes. • Entitled to favorable treatment upon distribution of gains from the disposal of assets with a minimum holding period of 12 months (long-term capital gains). *Foreign funds:* Treaty entitlement (credit or refund for U.S. withholding tax) usually under following conditions: • Funds are located in the contracting state. • The tax legislation of the contracting state may impose a tax on the funds income. • The economic ownership of the fund is mainly owned by individual persons operating in the contracting state.
Crediting of withholding taxes at asset level	N/A.
Distribution obligation for taxation reasons	Obligation to distribute at least 90 % of the taxable interest and dividends income.
Withholding tax (tax rate)	No.

(continued)

Specific characteristics of foreign assets/investors	*Foreign assets:* Entitlement to credit of foreign withholding tax can be transferred to the investors under the following circumstances: • Fund assets have to present 50 % shareholdings in foreign corporations at the end of the tax year. • Pass of the general conduit test in accordance with IRC Sect. 852. • Adherence of certain holding periods: Sect. 901 (k) and IRC Sect. 853 (c). • The actual distribution has to be increased by the foreign tax at investor level. The foreign taxes can be credited against the according income tax. *Foreign investors:* Deduction of withholding tax: • Dividends, interest and capital gains/refund of assets and fund shares (maximum holding period of 12 months) (30 %). • Capital gains from the disposal/refund of fund shares (minimum holding period: 12 months), if the investor resided at least 183 days a year in the U.S. (30 %). • Withholding tax deduction for the application of double tax agreement: from 0 % to 25 %.

Taxation at Investor Level

Distributed interest/dividends (tax rate)	*RIC*[a]: Taxable. Interest, dividends and capital gains treated as dividends resulting from the disposal of short-term assets (10 %, 15 %, 25 %, 28 %, 33 %, 35 %)[b].
Distributed capital gains (tax rate)	*RIC*[a]: • Taxable: capital gains from the disposal of fund shares (minimum holding period: 12 months) (10 %, 15 %, 25 %, 28 %, 33 %, 35 %)[b]; capital gains from disposal of long-term assets (from 0 % to 15 %). • Possibility to credit the already accrued taxes for retained capital gains.
Accumulated interest/dividends (tax rate)	Not taxable.
Accumulated capital gains (tax rate)	• Taxable: capital gains from the disposal of fund shares (minimum holding period: 12 months) (10 %, 15 %, 25 %, 28 %, 33 %, 35 %)[b]; capital gains from disposal of long-term assets (from 0 % to 15 %). • Possibility to credit the already accrued taxes for retained capital gains at the further distribution.
Consideration of the withholding taxes withheld at the domestic asset level	N/A.
Consideration of the withholding taxes withheld at the foreign asset level	Yes, creditable, if entitlement to credit is forwarded by RIC. Deduction of the US tax is limited to the foreign income.
Consideration of the withholding taxes withheld at the domestic fund level	N/A.
Consideration of the withholding taxes withheld at the foreign fund level	In general the investor should be entitled to a credit for the withholding tax suffered.

(continued)

Special characteristics of the foreign fund	*Consideration of the withholding taxes withheld at the foreign asset level:*
	If the US investor invests in an offshore entity that is treated as an "entity" in the US then the US investor would not be entitled to a tax credit for withholding tax suffered at the entity level—its income would be reduced by the withholding tax suffered. Where the offshore entity is a flow through vehicle (e.g. has made a check the box election to be treated as transparent from a US tax perspective), then generally the investor may be entitled to a tax credit for withholding tax suffered.
	Differentiation of foreign funds into three categories:
	PFIC (Passive Foreign Investment Company):
	• Two cumulative requirements:
	  – Test of income: At least 75 % of the gross income from the foreign investment company consists of dividends, interest income, license revenues (passive income).
	  – Test of assets: At least 50 % of the company assets consist of assets, which generate passive income.
	• Three alternative (option) tax systems for US investors in compliance with certain declaration obligations:
	  – No current taxation (general form): Upon receipt of a distribution, the fictive excess distributions[c] and capital gains are diversified ratably according to the days of fund shares' holding period and the applicable highest tax rate of the past time is determined. The previous tax amounts shall bear interest. Capital gains from the disposal of fund shares are additionally subject to taxation as ordinary gains.
	  – Current taxation by choice of QEF (Qualifying Electing Fund): The net income and net capital gains of the tax year are attributed to the investor regardless of distribution or retention and they are also subject to the current taxation. The classification of income depends on the underlying assets.
	  – Mark-to-market-taxation: Taxation of the annual surplus of the market prize through the annual adjusted historical costs of the fund shares.
	CFC (Controlled Foreign Corporation):
	• Two requirements:
	  – Fund shares need to be held by taxable investors in the USA in the amount of 50 %.
	  – Each investor must hold at least 10 % of shares.
	• Income is added to the taxable income, regardless of distribution or retention and it is subject to income tax as dividend (10–35 %).

(continued)

	• Possibility to credit the paid taxes from abroad. *FPC (Foreign Personal Holding Company):* • Requirement: More than 50 % of fund shares need to be owned by not more than 5 U.S. investors in the amount of 50 %. • Tax treatment: No information.
Profit from the disposal of fund shares (tax rate)	Taxable (15 %).

[a] Distributions of the fund are qualified either as dividends (interest income, dividend income, capital gains from the disposal of assets held not longer than 12 months) or as capital gains (capital gains from the disposal of assets held more than 12 months)
[b] Tax rate 2010. Assessment basis: $0–8,375, $8,376–34,000, $34,001–82,400, $82,401–171,850, $171,851–373,650, above $373,650
[c] Distributions of a tax year, accounting more than 125 % of the average distribution of the previous three tax years

3.2.12.2 Quantitative Comparison of Tax Burden for an American Investor

		Fund units in private property			
		Scenario 1 (capital expenditure 1,000,000 €)		Scenario 2 (capital expenditure 100,000 €)	
Country in which the fund is located: USA		Distribution	Retention	Distribution	Retention
Fund investing domestically	Stocks	21.77 %	N/A	17.35 %	N/A
	Bonds	22.92 %	N/A	18.34 %	N/A

Analysis

Since a US RIC is obliged to distribute at least 90 % of its taxable income (except for realised capital gains), the quantitative analysis is limited to the distribution case.

In both scenarios, our results indicate a slight advantage for the investment in an equity fund over the investment in a bond fund from a tax point of view. This result reflects the combined effect of the model assumptions and the progressive income tax rate. Although the equity fund considered here shows a higher return before tax (10.78 %) than the bond fund (6.00 %) and, consequently, the income derived from the equity fund is subject to a higher progression than that from the bond fund, the positive impact of the greater profitability superimposes the negative tax effect.

3.2.13 United Kingdom

3.2.13.1 Qualitative Description
Short Description of the Tax System

Unit Trust and OEIC Investments in a Unit Trust and an OEIC are treated identically taxwise. Both fund types are considered companies. They face an individual corporate tax of 20 % for accrued interest at fund level. Profits from the disposal of assets and dividends are tax free. The former are once again to be invested by the fund. Losses can be considered at fund level. Likewise, the consideration of withholding taxes takes place, in principle, at foreign asset level for the fund.

(continued)

3.2 Tabular Representation

The fund is in theory obliged to distribute the available net profits to the investors. For accumulations, the fund and investors are treated as if the earnings would have been distributed. On behalf of the investors, withholding taxes of 20 % for interest and 10 % for dividends are withheld at fund level. The classification of interest and dividends is determined by the proportion of fund assets in the so called "qualified assets". Withholding taxes can be considered within the scope of the individual taxation of the investor.

Distributed interest, dividends and capital gains are taxable. Interest faces a four tier tax rate from 10 % for taxable income up to £2,710, from 20 % for taxable income up to £34,370, from 40 % for taxable income up to £150,000 and from 50 % over this. For dividends the respective rates amount to 10 %, 32.5 % and 42.5 %, while the starting rate band (taxable income up to £2,710) is not applicable. Profits from the disposal of fund units are subjected to 18 % tax.

Regarding accumulated interest, a distribution at a certain time is assumed, so that the respective earnings are treated like distributed interest and dividends. Profits from the disposal of fund units are subjected to 18 % or 28 % taxation depending on the taxpayer's total taxable income. A 40 % taxation takes place in case of non-qualifying funds.

In respect of foreign investors in British funds or for investments in foreign funds by British investors, numerous specific points must be observed. Foreign investors face, in particular, no withholding tax for dividends. Foreign funds are distinguished between distributing and accumulated ones. Profits from the disposal of fund units in growth funds are taxed as income, so that the guidelines on the exemption for capital gains are not effective.

Basic Information and Sources of Law Concerning the Taxation of Funds

Description and basic characteristics	*AIF (Authorized Investment Fund):* • AUT (Authorized Unit Trust): common investment model; property is held in trust for the investors. • OEIC (Open-ended Investment Company): most common form. • QIS (Qualified Investor Scheme): – Sub form of AUT and OEIC. – Officially approved fund, which is available technically solely to sufficiently qualified investors. – Qualified investors are defined in COLL #8.1.3. – Fewer limitations for the operational and investment opportunities.
Investment supervision	Financial Services Authority (FSA).
Sources of law	• No separate investment tax law. • Guidelines for the tax treatment of earnings from investment assets are found in the following sources: – The Income and Corporation Taxes Act[a]. – The Financial Services and Markets Act[b]. – The Open-ended Investment Companies regulation[c]. – The Authorized Investment Funds Regulations[d]. – The FSA Regulations (COLL Handbooks).

[a]Last changed 1988
[b]Last changed 2000
[c]Last changed 2001
[d]Last changed 2006

Taxation at Fund Level

Method of income taxation (tax rate)	Individual corporation tax liability: • Dividends are tax exempt. • Interest is taxable (20 %). • Capital gains are tax free.
Consideration of losses	• Chronologically and amount dependent unlimited loss carry-forward. • Chronologically limited, but amount dependent unlimited loss carry-back.
Treaty access of the fund vehicle	*UK-Unit Trust and UK-OEIC:* • Generally has treaty access in respect of reduced tax rates and the crediting/refund potential. • As a result of the tax exemption for capital gains, the opportunity for the drawing down of benefits concerning the capital gains taxation in the double tax agreements is patchily laid out. *Foreign funds:* • Generally has treaty access under the following requirements: – Fund is considered to be resident in the contract partner's state. – Fund faces taxation in the contract partner's state[a]. • Consideration of withholding taxes takes place by crediting and/or refunding. • Foreign Trust-Structures which are based on British law: – Transparent entities. – Double tax agreements between the UK and the asset countries are decisive.[b]
Crediting of withholding taxes withheld at asset level	N/A.
Distribution obligation for taxation reasons	Yes, complete distribution of net earnings. If accumulated, funds are nevertheless treated as if all earnings would have been distributed (distribution notion).
Withholding tax (tax rate)	• Yes. • More than 60 % of the fund's means are invested in qualified assets[c]: Distributions qualify as interest (20 %). • At most 60 % of the fund's means are invested in qualified assets[d]: Distributions qualify as dividends (10 %).
Specific characteristics of foreign assets/investors	*Foreign assets:* Credit of foreign withholding taxes for British funds. *Foreign investors:* Distributions are partly taxable. The qualification of the earnings conforms to the investment objects: • Interest (more than 60 % of the fund asset is invested in qualified assets): – 20 % withholding tax. According to the stipulation of the double tax agreements between the investor's country of residence and the UK it is refundable. – Provided that the investor presents a non-residency certificate or invests via a trustworthy broker, a gross distribution takes place.

(continued)

3.2 Tabular Representation

	• Dividends (at most 60 % of the fund's means are invested in qualified assets): – No withholding taxation. – The tax credit of 1/9 of the net dividend can be refunded according to the stipulation of the double tax agreements between the investor's country of residence and the UK. • According to the stipulation of the double tax agreements between the investor's country of residence and the UK, the accrued corporate tax burden in the UK can be avoided at fund level through a cash settlement. The cash settlement is confined to the amount at which the tax credit of 1/9 of the distribution exceeds a corporate tax rate of 15 %.

[a]The Luxembourg and French SICAV do not have treaty access, because no tax liability exists at fund level
[b]Equally this applies for a French FCP which is seen as transparent
[c]Money, securities without company shares, investments in building societies, shares in qualified assets by investing AIFs
[d]Money, securities without company shares, investments in building societies, shares in qualified assets by investing AIFs

Taxation at Investor Level

Distributed interest/dividends (tax rate)	Taxable. Classification of earnings conforms to the underlying assets: interest (10 %, 20 %, 40 %, 50 %)[a], dividends (10 %, 32.5 %, 42.5 %)[a].
Distributed capital gains (tax rate)	Not taxable. Profits from the disposal of assets are reinvested in the fund.
Accumulated interest/dividends (tax rate)	Distribution information: • The total available amount for distribution is considered as distributed at a certain point in the distribution period. This period can be at most a year, but it is generally only 6 months. The payout point must be 4 months before the end of the period. • Notional distributions apply as British dividends and are taxed respectively (see distributed interest/dividends).
Accumulated capital gains (tax rate)	Not taxable. Profits from the disposal of assets are reinvested in the fund.
Consideration of the withholding taxes withheld at domestic asset level	N/A.
Consideration of the withholding taxes withheld at foreign asset level	If the fund was a corporate/opaque vehicle, the tax would be bourne by the fund entity and therefore the UK investors could not reclaim this withholding tax as the fund would act as a blocker. If the fund was a partnership/transparent vehicle, the UK investor could reclaim the withholding tax using the credit or deduction method.

(continued)

Consideration of the withholding taxes withheld at domestic fund level	• Dividends: – Yes. Credit, provided that the investor is personally tax liable. – Tax credit of 1/9 of the distribution amount. • Interest: Yes. Credit and if applicable refund (excess tax credit, investor is not taxable).
Consideration of the withholding taxes withheld at the foreign fund level	The UK investor could reclaim withholding tax using the credit or deduction method.
Special characteristics of the foreign funds	Classification into two categories: *Distributing* fund: • Distributions are taxed upon accrual. • Profits from the disposal of fund units are taxed as capital gains. • Deduction of withholding taxes withheld at the foreign asset level, if the foreign fund is considered transparent. Limit on British tax which is not applicable for these earnings. • If a distributing fund invests more than 5 % in an accumulating foreign fund, this fund qualifies as a growth fund. *Growth fund:* • To qualify as a distributing fund, the fund has to prove annually that it distributes 85 % of profits from the period and 85 % of the respective British profit. • Distributions are taxed upon accrual. • Profits from the disposal of fund units are taxed as income so that no guidelines amount to the exemption from capital gains. • Deduction of withholding taxes withheld at the foreign asset level, if the foreign fund is considered transparent. Limit on British tax which is not applicable for these earnings.
Profit from the disposal of fund units (tax rate)	*UK-Unit Trust and UK-OEIC:* Taxable (18 %/28 %). *Foreign fund:* Taxable (18 %/28 % or 40 %)[b].

[a]Tax rate 2012–2013. Basis for the taxation of interest: £0—2,710, £2,711—34,370, £34,371—150,000, over £150,000. Basis for the taxation of dividends: £0—34,370, £34,371—150,000, over £150,000

[b]Depends on whether the foreign fund is seen as a "qualifying offshore fund" or a "non-qualifying offshore fund"

3.2.13.2 Quantitative Comparison of Tax Burden for a British Investor

		Fund units in private property			
		Scenario 1 (capital expenditure 1,000,000 €)		Scenario 2 (capital expenditure 100,000 €)	
Country in which the fund is located: United Kingdom		Distribution	Retention	Distribution	Retention
Fund investing domestically	Stocks	17.90 %	33.50 %	15.59 %	31.14 %
	Bonds	36.60 %	44.22 %	32.54 %	39.05 %

Analysis

There are clear differences in tax burdens for all case constellations in both scenarios. In no situation is there a tax advantage to the British investor for investments in growth funds.

The advantage of distributing equity funds in comparison to cumulative equity funds is explained by the fact that in the latter case the principle of tax transparency is applied. As a result, in this case the investor has to pay high income taxes on deemed distributions (thereby crediting the taxes withheld at fund level) without the concerned earnings are actually distributed. Consequently, the investor suffers a strong negative time effect. Furthermore, in the retention alternative the income actually accumulated increases the returns realised by the fund in subsequent years which in turn boosts the income taxes payable by the investor. The same holds true for distributing and cumulative bond funds.

In case of bond funds, the advantage of the distributing is greater since at fund level retained earnings are subject to additional corporation tax. Besides the further burden on interest income at fund level, the higher taxation of interest income compared to dividend income at investor level results in a disadvantageous tax burden for cumulative bond funds.

The differences that occur between scenario 1 and 2 can be traced to the fact the income tax rate is progressive in nature which is why lower income, in relative terms, is taxed less.

References

Eichenberger O (2008) Individualbesteuerung der natürlichen Personen in der Schweiz - Modelle, Vor- und Nachteile sowie Alternativen. Dissertation, Universität St. Gallen. Haupt Verlag, Bern

Eidgenössische Steuerverwaltung (2010) Tabelle für die Berechnung der direkten Bundessteuer der natürlichen Personen (Art. 214 DBG). http://www.google.de/url?sa=t&source=web&cd=1&ved=0CBkQFjAA&url=http%3A%2F%2Fwww.estv.admin.ch%2Fbundessteuer%2Fdokumentation%2F00242%2F00384%2Findex.html%3Flang%3Dde%26download%3DNHzLpZeg7t%2Clnp6I0NTU042l2Z6ln1acy4Zn4Z2qZpnO2Yuq2Z6gpJCDdn12e2ym162epYbg2c_JjKbNoKSn6A-&ei=IwEhTLDBFMKhOKaZmXI&usg=AFQjCNFPttGWCEaIeVGnqBCYtYw5Zd23nA. Accessed March 4, 2010

Finanzdirektion Steuerverwaltung Kanton Zug (2010) Steuerfüsse der Gemeinde des Kantons Zug für die Steuerjahre 2007–2010 in % der einfachen Steuer (100%). http://www.google.de/url?sa=t&source=web&cd=2&ved=0CBoQFjAB&url=http%3A%2F%2Fwww.zug.ch%2Fbehoerden%2Ffinanzdirektion%2Fsteuerverwaltung%2Fsteuerfuss%2Fsteuerfuesse-2007-2010%2Fat_download%2Ffile pdf&ei=FQAhTJX6FIKeOP_VwVg&usg=AFQjCNGMc5gQl5d68BSEeyC9nZuNIAAguQ. Accessed March 4, 2010

Schweizerische Steuerkonferenz (ed) (2009a) Die Einkommensteuer natürlicher Personen (Stand der Gesetzgebung: 1. Januar 2009) - Steuerinformationen Bern 2009. http://www.estv.admin.ch/dokumentation/00079/00080/00736/index.html#sprungmarke0_72. Accessed March 4, 2010

Schweizerische Steuerkonferenz (ed) (2009b) Das schweizerische Steuersystem - Bern 2009. http://www.estv.admin.ch/dokumentation/00079/00080/00660/01044/index.html?lang=de. Accessed March 4, 2010

Schweizerische Steuerkonferenz (ed) (2009c) Die Steuern von Bund, Kantonen und Gemeinden - Ein Kurzabriss über das schweizerische Steuersystem - Bern 2009. http://www.estv.admin.ch/dokumentation/00079/00080/00660/01044/index.html?lang=de. Accessed March 4, 2010

Printed by Books on Demand, Germany